Free Stuff

FOR

Collectors

ON THE

INTERNET

Judy Heim and Gloria Hansen

C&T PUBLISHING

Copyright © 2000 Judy Heim and Gloria Hansen
Developmental Editor: Barbara Kuhn
Technical Editors: Steve Cook and Vera Tobin
Cover and Book Design: Christina Jarumay
Illustration: Christina Jarumay
Book Production: Nancy Koerner

Library of Congress Cataloging-in-Publication Data

Heim, Judy.
    Free stuff for collectors on the Internet /
Judy Heim and Gloria Hansen. -- 2nd ed.
    p.   cm.
    ISBN 1-57120-096-7 (paper)
    1. Collectors and collecting--Computer network resources. 2. Free
material--Computer network resources. 3. Internet (Computer network)
I. Hansen, Gloria. II. Title.
    AM215.H45 2000
    025.06790132--dc21
                    99-050854
                    CIP

Published by C&T Publishing
P.O. Box 1456
Lafayette, California 94549

Printed in China
10 9 8 7 6 5 4 3 2 1

DEDICATION

We dedicate this book to our moms, Esther Kuplerski and Terri Patrowicz, who have given us some of the best memories of our lives by taking us shopping with them. They have taught us not only how to spot bargains from fifty paces, but also how to clean them up and position them properly on the coffee table. They've also taught us how to smuggle everything from Waterford crystal to antique chairs into the house so our husbands wouldn't see them, but that's another story. Without our moms, our homes wouldn't be crammed with half the amount of stuff that they are—nor would our hearts. Thanks, Mom!

We'd also like to thank the antiquers, collectors, and garage-sale hounds who share so generously of themselves and their wisdom on the Web. By sharing their knowledge, they help educate others and make collecting more fun for everyone.

There are thousands of Web sites for collectors. Sifting through them was a challenge. While we've tried to select sites that we think offer the most valuable collecting advice, that doesn't mean there aren't many more out there that are equally illuminating. Also, because of the fluid nature of the Internet, it is inevitable that some of the Web sites in this book may have moved or even vanished. Had we included only those Web sites that are sure to be around many moons from now, this book wouldn't be nearly as valuable. We hope the Web sites in this book will get you started discovering all the information—and fun—that awaits you on the Web.

Symbols in this book

 You can find lots of free goodies on the Web, but you'll learn more if you follow the chat icons in the many discussion groups offered on the Internet.

 This icon signifies a bit of Judy-and-Gloria hard-earned wisdom—in other words, something we wished we knew when we first started cruising the Web.

 When you see this icon, read carefully—and don't make one of the same silly mistakes we have!

Table of Contents

CHAPTER 1

Indulge Your Collecting Passion on the Web

Y ou can buy anything on the Web. And we mean *anything*! Do you lust after antique samplers? Have a hankering for 19th century Finnish nautical prints or Norman Rockwell plates from the '80s? Maybe you finally have the cash to buy all the missing pieces for your Franklin Mint Civil War chess set. Maybe you're searching for "little glass danglies" to replace the ones on the vintage lamp your dog broke. Anything you desire— from any era in history—is probably out there somewhere on the Web waiting for you.

On the Web you can:

- Shop Web sites devoted to your favorite collectible. Browse auction sites for collectibles and antiques.

- Join discussion groups devoted to your collecting passion. No matter how specialized or obscure your collecting interest, there are probably at least a few discussion groups for it swirling through cyberspace. (There are even cyber-klatches devoted to collecting old tractors!)

- Tap into expert advice on caring for your collectibles, including storage, cleaning, and restoration help.

- Research the value of your collection.

- Find information to help you date collection pieces.

- Track down hard-to-find, long-desired collectibles.

- Unload the dust collectors on your shelves easily through Web fleamarkets, or your own Web site.

THE WEB IS A GIANT GARAGE SALE, BUT HOW DO YOU FIND ANYTHING?

Unfortunately, you can't type "Beanie Baby" into a Web searcher like **Altavista** (**http://www.altavista.com**) and come up with a great deal on Bubbles the Beanie Fish. Nor will you find that old 1976 Camero glove compartment you need by heading to a random newsgroup and posting a classified.

Similar to pre-cyber days, when "antiquing" meant hunting out quaint curio shops with yellowed dress forms in the window, you need to visit the little mom-and-pop Web pages with names like Aunt Flo's Elvis-O-Rama. You need to stroll the aisles of the Web fleamarkets like eBay (**http://www.ebay.com**). It even helps to network with other devotees of Mickey Mouse cookie jars (or whatever it is you seek). It takes a bit of poking around the Web to find the collectibles and the discussion groups you need.

That's why we've written this little guide. The collector's world in cyberspace is an expanding universe of homey Web pages and private—but valuable—discussion groups. Web fleamarkets sprawl everywhere. This book will show you how to tap in and find that cyber-klatch devoted to, say, *Titanic* movie memorabilia or the best spot to shop for bicycle chains from the '50s. It will speed you to resources that will help you care for, restore, and even sell items. We'll even give you advice on how to avoid being taken by hucksters.

Even Sotheby's is on the Web. You can peruse its auction catalog, look up auction results, and read features on topics like "What Is American Folkart?" You can even print a form to mail to Sotheby's to request a free appraisal of a family heirloom. Alas, they told us that our heirloom painting in the gilded frame would not even sell in their "arcade" division. ("Arcade" is Sotheby-speak for "bargain basement.")

⬢ THE WEB IS REVOLUTIONIZING THE WORLD OF COLLECTING

The easy accessibility of collectibles on the Web has turned more of us into collectors—many of us unintentional ones. Just a few years ago, in order to sell your old Barbie, you needed to run an ad in a collector's magazine or spend a weekend at a Barbie lovers convention. Now you can do it with just a few flicks of computer keys. Similarly, that's all you need to do to outfit your Jackie-O "Bubblecut" Barbie with new neon plastic mules.

The Web is profoundly influencing collectible prices—and the desirability of certain collectibles. On Web auctions, collectors bid up prices of collectibles that bear designer names or logos that might not have ordinarily commanded high prices. When bidding on things you can't touch, manufacturers' logos on glass, dolls, jewelry or whatever become critical signs of the item's quality. At the high end, auction houses report that rare items that collectors previously snapped up at high bids occasionally sell for less because savvy collectors realize that, rare as that item may be, it will very likely appear on the Internet sometime in the future. In other words, it's no longer as rare as it was once considered to be. Fate will probably give the bidders another chance to buy it, hopefully when their pocketbooks are healthier.

The Web is making its economic presence felt at the garage-sale level too. A collector of antique lightbulbs we know despairs, "Now that everyone is grabbing up everything imaginable at garage sales and selling it on eBay, I have a harder time finding lightbulbs. And I have to pay higher prices for the few I find!" From Internet discussion groups for antiquers, we know of several dealers who cruise garage sales Friday mornings in our own neighborhoods—and usually have their finds posted for sale on eBay by the end of the day!

Web auction sites like eBay have transformed the world of collecting, much to many garage sale pickers' despair. Yes, we often see people unloading household goods from their grandmother's estate on eBay—or so they claim.

Tips for Viewing Collectibles on Web Auctions with AOL

Clear Up Smeary Pictures—If you use Internet Explorer 5 to surf the Web with AOL, you may have noticed that IE 5 sometimes has problems displaying Web graphics. The culprit is AOL's graphics compression. Turn it off by heading to **My AOL/Preferences** and clicking the **WWW** icon. Head to the **Web Graphics** tab and remove the check beside "Use compressed graphics." Click **Apply**.

Clean Out Your Cache—Clean out AOL's cache directories and files regularly to keep the software from slowing down on the Web. Click **My AOL**, select **Preferences**, and click **WWW**. Under the **General** tab, click **Delete Files** under **Temporary Internet Files**; under **History** click the **Clear History** button. While you're there, click the **Settings** button under **Temporary Internet Files** and reduce the "amount of disk space to use" to store Web graphics to about 50 megabytes. A large cache file can slow down your Web sessions. Run Scandisk weekly.

Try a Different Browser—If you'd rather surf the Web with Microsoft's **Internet Explorer** or **Netscape**, once you connect to AOL, minimize the AOL software and fire up your favorite browser instead.

Power Down to AOL 3.0—If AOL's software seems to run slowly on your PC and if you have an older computer—a 486 or an older Pentium (or System 7.5 or under on a Mac), try installing an older version of AOL's software. You can download AOL 3.0 from AOL's Web site (**http://www.aol.com**).

AMERICA ONLINE IS A GOOD PLACE TO GET STARTED IF YOU'VE NEVER BEEN ONLINE BEFORE

AOL is a great way to get started on the Internet if you've never tapped into cyberspace before. But if you plan to sell collectibles, either through an auction site or your own Web site, you'll want to shop for an Internet service instead so that your customers can view product pictures on your Web shop as quickly as possible as they shop.

You can get a free startup disk by calling 800/827-6364, or have a friend download the software for you from **America Online**'s Web site (**http://www.aol.com**). The software is also preloaded on many new systems, including the iMac (which Gloria's mom proudly owns).

Once you've installed the software and have connected to America Online press **Ctrl-K** (or ⌘-**K** on a Mac), type the keyword **internet<enter>** or **web<enter>**, and you're on the Internet.

Among AOL's disadvantages are its hourly fees to access some areas of the service and the fact that the service's access numbers are long-distance calls for some. Also, AOL's numbers are sometimes busy in the evening (when all the kids are online). AOL also charges additional hourly access fees for anyone connecting from outside the continental United States or anyone calling through an AOL 800 number.

*Use the keyword: **antiques** to get to the antiquers forum on AOL. You'll find message boards, classifieds, and other features.*

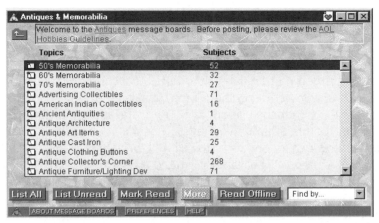

AOL hosts numerous message areas for collectors. The most popular are the ones devoted to hatpins and military memorabilia. These message boards aren't as active as the discussion groups for collectors you'll find elsewhere on the Internet.

IF YOU PLAN TO SELL COLLECTIBLES, HUNT FOR A LOCAL INTERNET SERVICE

Many people graduate from AOL to an Internet service provider (ISP) with local access numbers because of the better speed and reliability an ISP gives them and their customers. Whether you sign up with a national ISP or a local one, shop for one with a fast connection (at T1 speeds or better) directly into the Internet's network backbone and 56K bps connections that support the same connection standard as your modem does. Ask friends and neighbors for recommendations. You don't want an ISP that inflicts busy signals or is slow at delivering e-mail.

Most ISPs offer unlimited Internet access for $20/month. That usually includes the ability to set up a Web site. The amount of disk space you'll need will depend upon how many items you have up for sale at a given time. Five megs should get you started. You'll probably want a little storefront and a Web site where you can post scans of both your auction listings and items you may have for sale. Antiquers on the Net usually find that a combination of both is a good sales strategy. You don't need a fancy Web site, unless you start getting lots of orders.

Our picks for favorite national ISPs are AT&T's WorldNet **(http://www.att.net)** *and* Earthlink **(http://www.earthlink.com).**

Cable TV Offers High Speed Internet, But at a Price

Many local cable TV franchises offer Internet access through the same cable that sends you cable TV. With advertised connect rates of 10 megabytes per second, it's no wonder that cable Internet is getting popular—although actual connect rates are considerably lower depending upon what time of day you tap in. Cable Internet costs about $150 for installation, plus $40 to $50 per month. (That may be a good deal if you're getting gouged by local phone rates to call AOL or an ISP.) Cable Internet is presently available in limited areas of the country, though access is sure to grow. To find out if you can get it call your local cable TV franchise. Be sure to ask if there are any specials for new subscribers.

When you call for prices ask how many outlets are included in the installation fee (cable TVs and cable modems can't connect to the same outlet), and make sure you can actually connect to the Internet before your cable installer leaves. You'll also need to find out if you get any space for a Web site; many cable companies don't offer the ability to set up a Web site.

Some people use a combination of America Online and cable access. If you decide to go this route sign up for AOL's "Bring Your Own Access" subscription option for the cheapest rate.

Satellite Is Pricey,
But the Only Option in Some Rural Areas

If phone calls to the nearest ISP are eating into your lifestyle and cable Internet isn't available in your area, consider accessing the Internet via satellite. The main requirements are a Windows 95 or NT-running PC, a direct line of sight to the southern horizon, and a lot of patience. Hughes Network System's DirecPC (**http://www.direcpc.com**) is the leading satellite Internet service.

WHAT ABOUT "FREE E-MAIL" SERVICES?

There are two sorts of free e-mail services. First, there is **Juno** (**http://www.juno.com**), which gives you free software that you use to dial local access numbers and send and retrieve mail. Second, there are Web-based services like Microsoft's **Hotmail** (**http://www.hotmail.com**). You tap into these Web services through a computer that already has some Internet access—a work computer for instance, or one at a library or cyber-cafe. Their advantage is that you can send and retrieve private e-mail through the service without using, for instance, your work e-mail address when you tap in through your work computer.

Juno is a great deal, especially if there's a local access number in your area. But all you get is e-mail, unless you pony up $20/month for Web access.

> ✋ ***Warning!*** *There are disadvantages to using the "free e-mail" services like Juno and Hotmail. People who sell stuff on Web auction sites are not fond of dealing with people with "temporary" free e-mail addresses. In fact, it's not advised that you buy stuff from people with these free e-mail addresses, since the addresses are untraceable. Also, you may not be able to participate in some of the high-volume collectibles discussion mailing lists. These lists generate lots of e-mail each day—so much mail that it will quickly fill up your mail box on these services, causing the mailing list owner to unsubscribe you in irritation. In fact, some mailing lists won't even permit people who are using free e-mail services like Hotmail or Yahoo. It's best to subscribe to a "real" e-mail account with an ISP or online service like America Online.*

WHAT COLLECTORS NEED TO KNOW ABOUT THEIR WEB BROWSER

Whether you tap into the Web through an Internet service or America Online, the software centerpiece of your Web surfing is what's called a browser. In the old days different sorts of software did different things on the Net. For instance, you needed mail software to send and receive e-mail; a newsreader to read public discussions; you needed special software called FTP (for "file download protocol") to download files to your computer. Plus, you needed a browser to view (or browse through) the graphical portion of the Internet known as the Web. Now all those functions are built into browsers.

Most computers are sold with Netscape's Navigator or Microsoft's Internet Explorer already installed. You can also download them for free from **Netscape**'s Web site (**http://www.netscape.com**) or **Microsoft**'s (**http://www.microsoft.com**).

While you can use just about any computer to log onto the Internet in some fashion (even an original Apple II, circa 1979), to be able to view graphics you'll need a computer manufactured in at least the last eight years. If you have an older computer, download a copy of the $35 **Opera** browser (**http://www.operasoftware.com**) which will run on Windows 3.x-running PCs (as old as 386SX's) with 6 megabytes of RAM.

If you're running an older Macintosh, head to Chris Adams's **Web Browsers for Antique Macs** web page (**http://www.edprint.demon.co.uk/se/macweb.html**) and download **Tradewave's MacWeb** or an early version of **NCSA Mosaic**.

If you've never configured Internet software before, you'll need someone to help you, even if you're a computer genius (believe us, we know). Your ISP will (or should) give you directions on how to set up Windows 95 or the Macintosh OS to at least log on to their service.

But once you're connected, you're pretty much on your own. That's why we've put together this little tutorial.

*(**Note:** The following directions are for the latest versions of Explorer and Navigator, but, with the exception of the instructions for e-mail, most will work with earlier versions of the browsers.)*

HOW TO TAP INTO A WEB PAGE

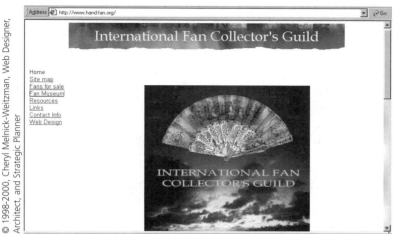

To get to a Web page, such as that of the **International Fan Collector's Guild**, type its address (also known as its URL, or Universal Resource Locator) into the **Address:** bar in Navigator, or the **Location:** bar in Internet Explorer

Take note that the case of the letters is important.

You can also cut and paste URLs from other documents into the address or location bar. Highlight the address with your mouse, press **Ctrl-C** (or ⌘-**C** on a Mac), then place the mouse in the location bar and press **Ctrl-V** (or ⌘-**V** on a Mac) to paste it in. Then hit **<Enter>**.

To move to other pages in the Web site, click on highlighted words, or, whenever your mouse cursor changes into a hand when its positioned on an object, right-click your mouse to go there.

Home
Site map
Fans for sale
Fan Museum
Resources
Links
Contact Info
Web Design

How to Find the Web Site if the Web Page Isn't There

URLs point you to directories on a remote computer just like directory paths (**c:\windows\programs**) get you to different directories and subdirectories on your computer's hard disk.

If a Web address doesn't get you to what you want, try working back through the URL. For example,

AntiqueRestorers.Com offers a library of articles about restoring furniture at:

http://www.antiquerestorers.com/Articles/FURNITURE_AR TICLES.htm

If it's not there when you get there, try:

http://www.antiquerestorers.com/Articles

Should that URL fail to display anything worthwhile, or if you get another error message, try AntiqueRestorer's home page at the URL root at:

http://www.antiquerestorers.com

If you get you to a directory that lists files like this, you can click on the highlighted names to view or even download them. If you see a file

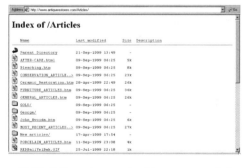

with an "HTM" or "HTML" at the end of its name, click on it. That's a Web page document. If it has a **.GIF** or **.JPEG** extension, it's a picture. If you get an error message like "Access denied," try going further back through the URL.

⚫ FIND YOUR WAY AROUND ON THE WEB WITHOUT GETTING LOST

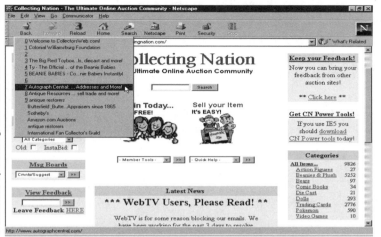

Right-click on the **Back** button in your browser for a list of Web sites you've recently visited. Click on their names to return to them.
• Click the **Back** button in your browser to return to previously visited Web sites.
• Click the **History** button or select the history feature from a drop-down menu to list previously visited URLs

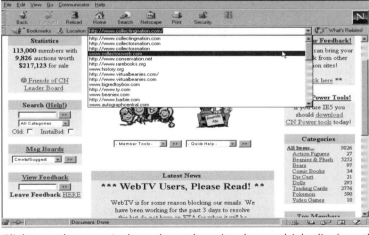

Click your browser's drop-down location box, which displays the last dozen or so URLs that you have actually typed into the browser (in other words, it doesn't display links that you've clicked on something to get to).

COMMON ERROR MESSAGES
WHEN YOU ENTER A WEB ADDRESS

 404 Not Found
The requested URL /blocks/tips.html was not found on this server.

Reason: Your browser was able to find the Internet service or the computer on which the Web site was or is hosted, but no such page was found on the service. (The very last "word" at the end of a URL is the page's address. For example, "tips.html.") Maybe the Web site owner removed that particular page. Or perhaps the Web site no longer exists.

Fix: Try working back through the URL as explained on page 16, to see if you can locate the Web site, or determine if the site itself is gone from the service. Also, try suffixing the page's address with "htm" or "html" instead of its current extension. For example, in place of tips.html, type tips.htm. (An HTML suffix is the same as an HTM, but some Web page hosting services require that Web pages be named with one or the other. Typing the wrong extension is a common mistake.)

 DNS Lookup Failure
or
Unable to locate the server.
The server does not have a DNS entry.
Reason: DNS stands for "domain name server." A domain name is the first part of a URL—for instance, in **www.ctpub.com**, **ctpub.com** is the domain name. Every Internet service (and AOL) has a database of such Web page host addresses. When you type a URL, the first thing your browser does is tell your Internet service to look up the domain name in its database, to find out where it's located. If it can't find it, your Internet

service's computer may poll other domain name directories around the Internet to determine if any of them know where the domain name can be found. If none of them do, you may get the error message "DNS Lookup Failure."

Why can't they find the domain name? Maybe it no longer exists. Or perhaps it's so new that the domain name databases your Internet service uses can't find it. Sometimes you also get this error message when there's heavy traffic on the Internet. Your Internet service is taking too long to look up the name, so your browser errors out.

Fix: Try typing the URL into your browser later in the day. If you still get the error message, try the URL a few days, or even a week later. If you still get error messages, the domain name no longer exists.

No Response from Server

Reason: Your browser is unable to get a timely response from the Web site's host computer. This can be because of heavy traffic on the Internet or on the branch of the Internet you are traveling. It can be because the computer that's hosting the Web site is overloaded (everyone is tapping in). Or it can be because your Internet service is overloaded, or its own computers are experiencing slowdowns for technical reasons.

Fix: Try the URL again, either in a few minutes, or later in the day.

Server Is Busy

Reason: A common error message issued by Barbie.Com and other heavily trafficked collectibles Web sites, it means that too many people are trying to tap in.

Fix: Try accessing the Web site later.

HOW TO USE BOOKMARKS

Web browsers let you "bookmark" sites so that you can visit them again simply by fishing through your bookmark catalog. You usually just click a bookmark icon (or Favorites in Internet Explorer)

To add a bookmark to Explorer click Favorites/Add to Favorites.

or select the feature from a toolbar to add to your bookmark list the Web site that you're currently visiting.

While a Web page is displayed, right-click on the page and from the pop-up menu select **Add Bookmark**.

You Can Add Shortcuts to Web Sites on Your Windows Desktop. Say there's a particular Web site you like to visit every day. If you're running Windows 95/98 you can add a shortcut to it from your desktop. When you click on the shortcut, your browser will load, dial your Internet service, and speed you to the Web site. Use your mouse to drag the site's URL from a link in a Web page. If you're using Internet Explorer, drag

Create buttons on your personal tool-bar in Netscape to whizz you to the Web sites you like to visit frequently. First, display the toolbar by pulling down the View

menu, selecting Show, and placing a check beside Personal Toolbar. Then, while the Web page is displayed, drag the Location icon to the Personal Toolbar just below.

The icon should look like this when you're successfully dragging the Web site's location to your toolbar.

Click this button whenever you want your browser to take you to the Butterfield & Butterfield Web site.

from the **Address** bar to the left of the **Links** bar or the **Favorites** menu. If you're using Netscape, drag the icon to the left of **Location:** when a page is loaded. Your mouse cursor should change into a circle with a slash as you drag the URL to the desktop.

You Can Customize Your Browser's Personal Toolbar by Adding Bookmarks. You can customize the personal toolbar in Communicator, or the **Links** bar in Internet Explorer by adding, not only icons for frequently visited URLs, but folders of bookmarks. In Communicator add a URL to the personal toolbar by dragging a link from a Web page or by dragging the icon to the left of **Location:** when a page is loaded. To add a folder instead to the personal toolbar click the **Bookmarks** icon, select **Edit Bookmarks** and highlight the folder you wish to place on the toolbar. Right-click and select **Set as Toolbar Folder**. In Internet Explorer you can similarly customize the **Links** bar by adding individual URLs as well as folders. Drag folders from the **Favorites** menu to add them to the **Links** bar.

To add a URL to the Links bar drag it from the **Address** bar to the left of the Links bar, from the **Favorites** menu or from a Web page.

You Can Use Third-Party Bookmark Software to Organize Your Bookmarks. There are a lot of low-cost utilities for organizing bookmarks that you can download from the Web. These are particularly handy if you're using two browsers—both Netscape and Internet Explorer for example. They enable you to store your bookmarks in a central location, and organize them into folders with icons—and in a more efficient manner than you can in your browser. Some utilities also let you password protect bookmarks. A good spot to download them is C/net's **Shareware.Com** (**http://www.shareware.com**). Search for the phrase "bookmark organizer." For PCs, one we like is the $29 shareware program **LinkMan Professional** from Thomas Reimann. For Macs we like **URL Manager Pro**, the $25 shareware program from Alco Blom (**http://www.url-manager.com**).

There are tens of thousands of Usenet newsgroups. You can't scroll through the whole list looking for discussion groups in your interests. But here are some good keywords to use to search the list: **collect, antiques, toys, vintage, fan**. You should also search with words in your interests: **beanie, plushie, Star Trek**, etc.

⬤ PRINTING WEB PAGES AND SAVING PICTURES TO DISK

When you're shopping on the Web you're often going to want to print the page that displays the auction offering—or save a picture of it to your disk to examine later.

To Print a Web Page

From your browser's menu select **Print**. If the page has frames you may need to first click on the frame that you want to print in order to select it. From the File menu, select **Page Setup** if you want to print the URL or date on the page (this feature is available only in newer browsers). If you're using a Macintosh, try the $10 shareware program **Net-Print** from John Moe (**http://www93.pair.com/johnmoe**), which allows you to print whatever text you select, rather than the entire page.

To Save a Picture to Disk

Position your cursor over the image and right-click. On a Mac, click-hold. A menu box will pop up. Select **Save Image As...** or **Save Picture As...** You can later view it in either your browser or a graphics program like Paint Shop Pro.

Can't Find a Picture That You've Saved to Your Disk? It happens all the time. You click on an image on the Web to save it to your computer, then you can't find it. If you can't remember the name of the graphic that you saved, go back to the Web page and click on it again to see the name. Then, if you have a PC running Windows 95/98, click **Start**, then **Find** and type the name of the file. Windows will find it for you. If you have a Mac with an operating system of 8.5 or higher, go to the Apple menu and launch **Sherlock**. Click **Find File** and type in the name of the file.

Judy & Gloria's Ten-Step Program for Fixing Browser and Graphics Crashes

After you spend an hour or so clicking around an auction or collectibles Web site, your browser may start acting—well, flaky. Maybe Web pages stop appearing so quickly or your computer grinds its disk a lot. Maybe your PC just locks up. Any number of things could be causing the problem. Follow these steps to make your life browser crash-free:

STEP 1. Cold boot the PC. In other words, shut down your software, turn the power off, and turn it back on a few minutes later when the disk stops spinning. That will clean any flotsam out of its memory. Your browser will be flying again when you log back on the Web, but this solution is only temporary. Some people reboot their PC several times in the course of an evening. We think that's unnecessary. That's why we recommend the next steps.

STEP 2. Head to the Web sites of the maker of your PC, its video card, and its modem, and download any fixes or new drivers.

Step 3. Clean up your hard disk by running Scandisk and Disk Defragmenter. Click **Start/Programs/ Accessories/System Tools**. (You should do this every few weeks.) On a Mac, use **Disktools**, available in the Extras folder on your operating system CD.

STEP 4. If you're running Windows 95/98, head to Microsoft's Web site (**http://www.microsoft.com**) and download any new fixes, patches, or upgrades. (There are always fixes to download for Windows.) While you're there, download the current version of Internet Explorer and any fixes for that too, if that's the browser you run. If you use Netscape, get the newest one of that (**http://www.netscape.com**).

STEP 5. If you're running a version of AOL 3.0 earlier than 131.75, you need to upgrade. For AOL 4.0, upgrade if it's lower than 134.224. If you're running Windows 95 (or System 7.5 or earlier) and experiencing crashes with AOL 4.0 you might want to return to using AOL 3.0. Use the keyword "upgrade." To find out what version of AOL you're running click **Help/About America Online**. Hit **Ctrl-R** when the AOL window pops up. To find out what version of AOL you're using on a Mac, launch AOL, and select **About AOL** under the Apple menu.

STEP 6. A surfing browser will push your computer's memory to the limit. Try shutting down unnecessary applications while surfing and see if that helps. Press **Ctrl-Alt-Delete** to get a list of applications and close down everything but Explorer, Systray and your browser. On a Mac, click the **Finder Application Icon** and Quit any unneeded programs. To troubleshoot your PC system further, right-click on **My Computer** and choose **Properties**. In the **Device Manager** tab make sure that no red or yellow flags signal hardware conflicts. In the **Performance** tab make sure that System Resources scores at least 85% free. Click the **Virtual Memory** button and select "Let Windows manage my virtual memory settings." Click **OK**. If AOL's crashing you should try shutting down your virus software to see if that might be the source of the conflict.

STEP 7. Your browser needs lots of disk space for its cache. At least 50 megabytes, or 10 percent of your disk should be free. You should empty your browser's cache weekly. Delete Netscape's history file (**netscape.hst**) and Cache folder. Clean out AOL's cache by heading to **My AOL/Preferences/WWW**. Head to the **General** tab and click the **Delete Files** and **Clear History** buttons. For Explorer delete the folder **Temporary Internet Files** found in the Windows directory.

STEP 8. If Web page pictures look smeary or if your computer locks up while you're scrolling down a page, your video driver or graphics card may be at fault. Right-click on an empty spot in the desktop, click Properties. In the **Settings** tab change the **Colors** to 256. Click Apply. Under the **Performance** tab move down the **Hardware Acceleration** slider a notch. Click **OK**.

STEP 9. If your browser crashes while printing Web pages, it may be because your printer needs an updated driver. Or, it might need a bidirectional cable. Most printers are sold with bidirectional cables these days, but there's always that odd duck. But try this first: head to the **Control Panel,** click the **Printer** icon, and right-click on the icon for your printer. **Select Properties**. In the **Details** tab select **Spool Settings**. Set **Print** direct to printer. If there's an option to disable bidirectional support, do it.

STEP 10. If you think Netscape is at fault, head to Netscape's crash troubleshooting page (**http://help.netscape.com/kb/client/970203-1.html**). If you think Explorer is at fault, write down the Invalid Page Fault error message it spits out then search for the message on Microsoft's tech support site (**http://www.microsoft.com/support**). Better yet, search for the names of your computer, your graphics card, and your modem on both Web sites. The chances are very good that you'll find your solution on one of them.

Mac User Alert! If AOL crashes too often, a corrupt AOL Preferences file in the System Folder may be to blame. Quit AOL, then open the **System Folder/Preferences/ AOL/Preferences**. Drag only the **AOL Preferences** file to the trash. Then relaunch AOL. The program will create a new preference file in the System File.

Here are more things to try:

If you're feeling ambitious, download a new version of your browser, then uninstall your old one (this step is important). Then reinstall the new one.

• If Explorer spits out a Java or ActiveX error while trying to display a Web site, then it goes belly up, try disabling these scripting languages. From the **Tools** menu select **Internet Options**. Head to the **Security** tab and click the **Internet** icon. Click dots beside **Disable** in these categories: Download signed ActiveX controls; Run ActiveX controls and plugins; Active Scripting; and Scripting of Java applets. Under **Java** select **Disable Java**.

• If AOL is the source of your woes (the sign that the problem lays with your AOL software and not too many people logging on to the AOL network is that AOL freezes without the hourglass symbol), try deleting the AOL Adapter. From the **Start** menu select **Settings**, then **Control Panel**. Click the **Network** icon and head to the **Configuration** tab. Highlight "AOL Adapter" and click Remove. Restart Windows. Sign back on to AOL and AOL will reinstall an updated version of the adapter.

• Try calling a different AOL number and see if that remedies the freeze-ups. Head to **My AOL/Access Numbers** to find a new number.

• Use the keywords "Members Helping Members" to find up-to-date solutions to AOL freeze-ups.

HOW TO SEND E-MAIL

If you're using America Online all you need to do is click on the **You Have Mail** icon on the greeting screen to read your e-mail or send mail, even out on the Internet. (To send messages to someone on the Internet from AOL type the full Internet address—for example **info@ctpub.com**—into the **To:** line in the AOL mail screen, just as you'd type an AOL address.)

If you're using an Internet service you can use special mail software like **Eudora** or **Pegasus**. Or, you can use the mail program built into your browser.

In Navigator, press **Ctrl-2** to get to Messenger, the mail program. On a Mac, click the **Mail** icon box in the lower right-hand corner of the browser's screen to get to your in-box. The keystroke ⌘-T retrieves new e-mail.

In Explorer, click the **Mail** icon in your Windows 95/98 tray to load the Outlook Express mail program. On a Mac, click the **Mail** icon on your menu bar.

HOW TO READ USENET NEWSGROUPS WITH YOUR WEB BROWSER

Many talk groups for collectors swirl through that raucous amalgam of newsgroups known as Usenet. But tapping into them can be tricky. You need to set up your browser to download the groups from your Internet service, then use your browser's mail reader to read them.

The first time you want to read a newsgroup you'll need to download from your ISP a complete list of current newsgroups. Then you'll need to search it and subscribe to the groups you're interested in. Finally, you need to download the messages themselves. Here's how to do it with Netscape and Explorer:

 Warning to Parents! The Usenet newsgroups are unmoderated and uncensored. We spotted a lot of pornography in some of the collectors newsgroups, particularly ones for children's collectibles.

If You Can't Access a Web Page Try These Tricks:

If Netscape's logo keeps "snowing" but doesn't display any page, it may be because Netscape has frozen. Try accessing the Web site with Explorer instead. For convenience, cut the URL from Netscape's Location bar and paste it into Explorer's.

If you click on a highlighted link on a Web page but don't seem to get anywhere, try right-clicking on the link instead. From the pop-up box select "Open in New Window" or "Open Frame In New Window."

If you click to a Web page with Netscape and the Web page appears to be blank, try accessing it with Explorer instead. Netscape is fussy about certain types of coding on pages and may refuse to load a page because it choked on some bit of coding.

If a page doesn't appear to load properly, click the **Reload** button.

If you're running Internet Explorer 5 and occasionally Web pages load only partially, you need to download a patch from Microsoft's Web site (**http://www.microsoft.com**).

How to Read the Usenet Antique & Collectible Newsgroups with Netscape

1. You must first set up your browser to retrieve newsgroups from your Internet server. Find out from your Internet service the name of the computer where newsgroups are stored. (It will be something like **groups.myisp.com**.) Pull down the **Edit** menu and select Preferences. Under **Mail & Newsgroups**, head to the **Newsgroup Servers** or **Group Server** setup box and click Add. Type the name of your ISP's newsgroup server. Click OK to save it.

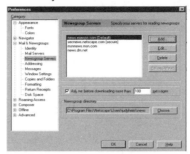

First you need to tell Navigator the name of the server on your ISP where newsgroups are stored.

2. Connect to your Internet service.

3. Head to Navigator's message center by pressing **Ctrl-2** or click the **Mail** icon box in the lower right-hand corner of the browser's screen on a Mac.

4. From the **File** menu, select **Subscribe to Discussion Groups**.

5. Click the **All** or **All Groups** tab to download a list of current newsgroups. This may take a while since the list is large. The message "Receiving discussion groups" should appear on the very bottom line of the screen. Hit the **Refresh List** button if you or someone else in your household has set up the news-reader to subscribe to mailing lists in the past.

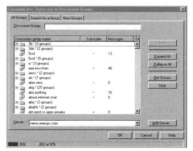

You need to download the complete list of newsgroups in order to search for the ones about collectibles.

6. When that humongous list of newsgroups has finished downloading, head to the **Search for a Group** tab. Type "antiques" or "collect" in the search box (or whatever you're interested in) and click the **Search Now** button.

7. Once the newsgroup searcher has come up with a list of interesting newsgroups, highlight the one you want to read, and press the **Subscribe** button. A check will appear beside it.

8. To read your newsgroup, head back to the message center (**Ctrl-2** or click the **Mail** icon box on a Mac). From the pull-down menu box at the top of the screen, select the newsgroup and click **Download Messages**. Or, click the **Get Msg** icon. You may want to download only a selection (under 500 for example) and mark as read the rest of the messages. This way, the next time you download messages from the newsgroup, you will only download the newest ones.

9. From the **Go** menu you can move from thread to thread, reading messages and skipping others.

10. In the future to read messages, go to the message center (**Ctrl-2** or click the **Mail** icon box on a Mac). From the pull-down menu box at the top of the screen, select the newsgroup you want to read. From the File menu select **Get Messages/New**.

After you download and search the newsgroups, subscribe to the groups you want to read by selecting them. You can click through the list just as you'd click through subdirectories on your computer.

Select the messages and message threads you want to read and they'll appear in the bottom of the screen. (If you don't get a split screen you may need to "pull up" the bottom portion of the screen with your mouse. In other words, the window is there, it's just hidden.)

How to Read the Usenet Antiques & Collectibles Newsgroups with Microsoft Explorer

1. Load the **Outlook Express** mail portion of Internet Explorer by clicking on the mailbox icon on the top right-hand corner of the screen. Click the **Read News** icon on the Express screen. If you have not yet set it up to read 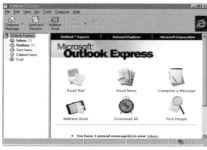 newsgroups with your ISP, a setup wizard will appear. It will prompt you for your name, e-mail address, and the name of the dial-up connection you use to connect to your ISP. Most important of all it will ask you the name of the server on your ISP where the news messages can be found.

2. The next time you click Express's **Read News** icon it will ask you if you'd like to download a list of the newsgroups from your ISP. This may take a while since there are tens of thousands of newsgroups.

✋ *Warning! If you try to download more than 500 news-group messages with Explorer it will crash.*

Read Usenet Collectibles Newsgroups from Your Browser You can read the collectibles newsgroups from the comfort of your Web browser by heading to **Dejanews** (**http://www.dejanews.com**). Reading them through this Web site isn't as easy as reading them with your browser's newsreader, but it's a simple way to access the groups.

TIPS FOR KEEPING CHILDREN SAFE ON THE WEB

*Be sure to supervise your children on the Net—*the best way is to talk to them regularly about what they're doing online. Warn them as often as you can not to meet in person strangers they may meet online, even if they insist the new friend is a teenager—sometimes they're not .

Keep the kids away from the Usenet news-groups where pornography is rife. If you're on AOL use the Parental Controls (keywords: **parental controls**) to block your child's access to Usenet. You should also block their screen name from receiving binary files (i.e. pictures) in e-mail.

3. Type "antiques" to search the list for news-groups that contain "antiques" in their name or "collect." Or "beanies" or whatever else you're interested in. Subscribe to them by highlighting each, clicking the **Subscribe** but-

ton. Then click **OK** when you're done. (Notice: there is even an alt.recovery.mania.beanies newsgroup!)

4. To read newsgroups that you've subscribed to, click the **Go To** button. Or, click on the name of the news-group on the left side of the screen. To read individ-ual messages, click on the headers displayed at the top right of the screen.

How to Read the Usenet Antiques & Collectibles Newsgroups on America Online

1. To read the Internet newsgroups through AOL press **Ctrl-K** or ⌘**-K** on a Mac and type the keyword: newsgroups. Click on the **Search All Newsgroups** icon to search the tens of thousands of newsgroups

for ones in your interests. (Some search words that work are: **antiques, collect, beanies,** etc.)

2. Once you click the **Search Newsgroups** icon, type your search word and press **Search**. Once AOL comes up with a list of matching newsgroups, click the **Add** button to add selected newsgroups

to the list of newsgroups that you wish to read, or click on the name of the newsgroup and from the pop-up box click "Subscribe to newsgroup." Depending upon which version of AOL's software you're using you can read the messages in the newly subscribed newsgroup immediately, or else you'll need to head back to the main newsgroup menu by closing the windows (click the X in the upper right-hand corner). Click the **Read My Newsgroups** button to pop up a list of the newsgroups to which you're subscribed. Click the **List Unread** button to list messages in the newsgroups that you have not yet read.

3. To read listed messages and their replies, highlight the message and click the **Read** button.

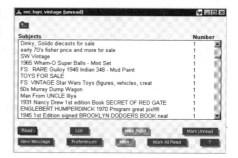

TIPS FOR STAYING SAFE ON THE WEB

The Internet is safer than the average subway station—but sometimes not by much. We know you're an adult and will take care of yourself just as you would in a subway station. But just so you know we're concerned about your safety, here are our motherly warnings:

• **Never give anyone your credit card, any of your online passwords, or any personal information** such as your street address or phone number. An all-too-common ruse is for hackers to e-mail a new subscriber to America Online alleging they are a representative of AOL and need the subscriber to resubmit their credit card number for verification. Another ploy is for hackers to claim they work for Microsoft and to e-mail victims a "security patch" for Internet Explorer. Once the "security patch" is installed it e-mails to the hackers the victim's passwords. No one ever e-mails a security patch!

• **Beware of get-rich-quick offers that arrive by the megabyte in your e-mail box.** And never answer junk e-mail. You'll either be bombarded with more e-mail, or the sender may retaliate if you ask to be removed from their mailing list. (That happened to a prominent woman in the craft industry. An angry junk e-mailer mail-bombed her company's e-mail server after she asked to be removed from his mailing list.)

• **If you shop on the Web, pay with a credit card in case there are problems**. Never type your credit card into any Web site that's not a "secure" Web site. That means that the site will encrypt the information you send it. As you enter a secure site your browser will tell you that it's secure. Also, Navigator will display a lock icon.

free Big Web Sites About Antiques & Collectibles

There are so many *great* Web sites for antiquers and collectible lovers. On them you can read features about collecting, find out what's hot, and chat with other collectors. You can learn how to research your collectible, find links to other Web sites that will help you determine prices of items in your collection, and find out how to care for your collection. The sites for collectors that we recommend in this chapter are the *big* Web sites. Use them as a starting point to get to the Web sites and discussion groups devoted to the things that you collect. For example, from the **About.Com** Web sites listed in this chapter below you can easily click your way to other wonderful About.Com Web centers devoted to doll and toy collecting, sports memorabilia, and many other collecting passions.

Head to the collectible and antique forums at About.Com to get started finding friends and information relevant to your collecting passion.

About.com - Collecting - Netscape

File Edit View Go Communicator Help

Bookmarks   Location: http://home.about.com/hobbies/collecting/

About.com™   collecting

expert guides to help you find/ learn/ share

Content: AboutToday | JustAbout
TalkAbout: Newsletters | Forums | Chat | Join
ShopAbout: ShopNow | Books | Videos | Yellow Pages

Sections About

Arts/Crafts
Collecting
Pastimes

Resources
Auctions
Gardening Week
Genealogy Tools

Subscribe to
About House and Home
and stay tuned to the House and Home news

Guide Sites

- Action Figure Collecting
- Barbie Doll Collecting
- Book Collecting
- Ceramic Arts
- Collectibles
- Comic Book Collecting
- Costume Jewelry Collecting
- Doll Collecting

- Kids' Collecting
- Mineral Collecting
- Miniatures
- Pin Collecting
- Sports Trading/Collect Cards
- Stamp Collecting
- Toy Collecting
- Vintage Cars

 Amassing Tomes A love of literature can be a hobby with Book Collecting Guide Cathy Gallagher.

 Wanna Trade? Kids' Collecting Guide Robert Olson has a goldmine of links.

Guide of the Day

 Bee Not Afraid: Get hip to bee culture, from your Beekeeping

COLLECTING AT ABOUT.COM
http://home.about.com/hobbies/collecting

About.Com forums are among our favorite places for reading salty opinions about the world of collectibles, finding good guidance and lots of how-tos, and chatting with other collectors.

From the main About.Com collecting Web page you can click your way to About.Com forums in the following collectible categories: action figures, Barbie dolls, dolls (general), book collecting, ceramic arts, collectibles in general, comic books, costume jewelry, kids' collecting, minerals, miniatures, pins, sports trading/collect cards, stamps, toys, and vintage cars.

ANTIQUES AT ABOUT.COM
http://antiques.about.com

Antique maven Pamela Wiggins is the host of this cyber-guide to antiquing on the Web, which has special feature stories, plus links to Web resources pertaining to your favorite types of antiques.

BARBARA CREW'S COLLECTIBLES AT ABOUT.COM
http://collectibles.about.com

No matter what you collect, you'll find lots of information about it in wonderful forums and libraries. Barbara writes about everything from Elvis to cookie jars, and shows you the way to all the best Web resources for your collecting passion. Her collecting how-tos are wonderful. Learn the ins and outs of shipping precious collectibles and keeping yourself from getting scammed on Web auction sites.

COLLECTIBLES AT SUITE101.COM
http://www.suite101.com/category.cfm/collecting

Suite101.Com offers "guide" sites similar to About.Com, with features, chat rooms, and links in the following collectible categories: antiques and collectibles, antique computers, Beanies, bottle collecting, doll collecting, doll repair, dollhouses and miniatures, model horses, lace making and collecting, toy collecting, and movie and TV memorabilia.

BARBARA NICHOLSON'S ANTIQUES & COLLECTIBLES AT SUITE101.COM

http://www.suite101.com/welcome.cfm/antiques_and_collectibles

Barbara offers articles, links, and discussion groups on antiques and collectibles. Her articles span an eclectic range from Biedermeier to 18th century furniture styles.

ANTIQUERESOURCES.COM

http://www.antiqueresources.com

Antique Resources offers a big library of how-to articles for anti-quers, plus links to antique malls around the Net and Web auction sites. This is a great spot to head to for late-night reading.

You can tap into a wide variety of collectible forums through Microsoft Network on the Web.

RON MCCOY'S COLLECTORS WEB

http://collectorsweb.com

You can read regular features, tap into message boards devoted to hundreds of categories of collectibles, plus read a newsletter. A great site!

DELPHI COLLECTING AND ANTIQUE FORUMS
http://www.delphi.com

The mega bulletin-board site Delphi offers hundreds of discussion areas devoted to different types of collectibles. To find them click the "Hobby and Craft" category on Delphi's main page.

Some topics covered include: Barbies, Hallmark ornaments, movie trailers, radio-controlled vehicles, stamps, Disney, Dept. 56 collectibles, dolls, phonographs, comic books, model railroads, Pfaltzgraff, Beanies, action figures, Strawberry Shortcake, Furbies, military memorabilia, Weebles, and more. Delphi hosts multiple discussion groups in many collectible categories, so be sure to search the complete list.

MICROSOFT NETWORK WEB COLLECTIBLE COMMUNITIES
http://communities.msn.com/collectibles

Microsoft Network offers a wide selection of forums on collectible topics. Anyone with a browser can tap in through the Web. Topics include: Beanies, dollhouses, Depression era glassware, Hummels, sports cards, Teddy bears, and antiques. Regular feature and links to other Web resources run in each of the forums. Online chatting is also available, although you need to be running Internet Explorer to tap in.

Looking for Web Sites that Sell Antiques and Collectibles? Head to **Curioscape** (**http://www.curioscape.com**) or the **Antique Searcher** (**http://www.antiquesearcher.com**) for a guide to Web stores. Other directories to check out are **Antique Hot Spots** (**http://www.antiquehotspots.com**) and **Antiques A-Z** (**http://www.booksatoz.com/AntiquesAtoZ**).

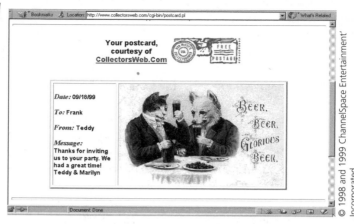

Send a Friend an Old-Fashioned Postcard Via E-mail

At **Collectors Web** you can send an old-fashioned postcard to a friend—for free. Select a postcard from dozens of antique cards and personalize it with your own message. Collectors Web will send an e-mail to your friend containing a URL where they can view their electronic greeting. Head to the **Collectors Web Postcard Page** (**http://collectorsweb.com/postcards/cardcenter.html**). Other Web sites for collectibles also offer free postcards, including **Virtual Beanies** (**http://www.virtual-beanies.com**) and **Wendy Gell Collectibles** (**http://www.wendygell.com**).

THE COLLECTINGCHANNEL.COM
http://www.collectingchannel.com

You'll find news, features and chat rooms for a variety of different collectibles. Topics for feature articles include: action figures, antiques, beanie stuff, books, coins, collectibles, comics, die-casts, dolls and bears, farm collectibles, garage, glass, jewelry, movie collectibles, music, pottery, sports collectibles, stamps, toys, TV and radio collectibles.

COLLECTOR'S UNIVERSE
http://www.collectorsuniverse.com

and

COLLECT.COM
http://www.collect.com

You'll find online feature stories on a variety of collectibles in Collector's Universe/Collect.Com. You'll also find free online price guides, glossaries, and discussion groups in the following categories: advertising, Americana, ancient coins, antiques, art, autographs, banknotes, beanies, books, cigars, modern coins, comic books, cowboy memorabilia, cigars, dolls, diamonds, glass, gold, silver, golf col-

lectibles, guitars, Indian collectibles, magazines, military, minerals, movie memorabilia, paper, photographs, porcelain, pottery, political collectibles, postcards, radio & TV collectibles, science-fiction collectibles, stamps, sports, surfing collectibles, toys, sports memorabilia, watches, trains, toys, and wine.

WORLD COLLECTORS NET
http://www.worldcollectorsnet.com

The site features news, features, and histories about leading collectibles in several dozen categories such as Royal Albert, buttons, Pez, Wedgwood, Furbys, Hallmark, and McDonalds. Each category features a message board (over 100 message boards total) and links to additional pages. Price Guides and Trends detail prices from observation at auctions, sales, and dealer sites. There's also a searchable collectibles directory.

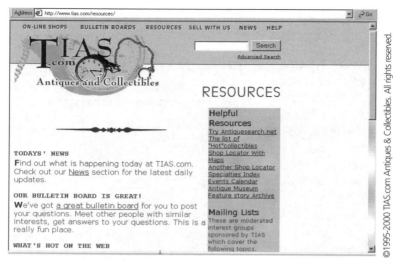

Click "Bulletin Boards" to read many wonderful conversations about collectibles and antiques.

THE INTERNET ANTIQUE SHOP
http://www.tias.com

TIAS is primarily a dealer Web site featuring many different Web-based antiques and collectibles dealers. If you click on "Bulletin Boards," you'll find a large and wonderful selection of collectibles, communities, and conversations. Click "Resources" to find a list of mailing list discussion groups sponsored by TIAS.

ANTIQUE WORLD
http://www.antiquesworld.co.uk/index.html

England's leading gateway to antique and collectibles information. You'll find guides to antique fairs throughout the UK, plus features on eclectic subjects ranging from Britain's hollow ground figures to Soviet porcelain.

free Help Getting Started Collecting

The day you realized that the Beanie Baby you picked up at an airport in Peoria has since multiplied into thirty felty creatures was the day you knew you'd crossed the line from casual shopper to serious collector. Whether you accumulate cat-shaped bean bags or cat-shaped earrings, there are Web sites out there to help you. They'll help you master the lingo (are cat-shaped earrings a collectible or an antique?). They'll help you strategize a purpose for your collection (do you plan to wear them, or just show them?). They'll even help you restore and display them. This chapter will take you to Web sites that offer antiques and collectibles glossaries, as well as those that offer tips for newbie collectors of different sorts.

"TEN SIMPLE TIPS TO REMEMBER AS YOU SHOP" FROM *COUNTRY LIVING MAGAZINE*
http://homearts.com/cl/collect/10tipsf1.htm

"Determine if what you are buying is as old as it is purported to be" is among the nuggets of good advice offered to aspiring collectors in this article from the magazine.

ANTIQUERESOURCES.COM GETTING STARTED FEATURES
http://www.antiqueresources.com/articles/index.html

Antique Resources offers many excellent features on getting started collecting all sorts of things—from fishing tackle to ancient coins.

JUDITH KATZ-SCHWARTZ'S ARTICLES ON COLLECTIBLES
http://www.msjudith.net/a&c.htm

Katz-Schwartz, a well-known appraiser and dealer at Twin Brooks Antiques, offers a wide variety of articles on her Web site for newcomers to collecting. "Driving Miss Grandma: What Really Constitutes a Collection?" is a memoir of her eccentric grand-mother, an antique wheeler and dealer extraordinaire. She also offers tips on buying at auctions, both tangible and in cyberspace, and much more.

"COLLECTING WITH A PURPOSE"
FROM *COUNTRY COLLECTIBLES MAGAZINE*
Are you a compulsive shopper, a connoisseur, or just plain crazy? Find out what kind of collector you are in this "self-help" guide.

COUNTRY LIVING MAGAZINE'S
COLLECTIBLE GUIDE
http://homearts.com/cl/toc/00clclc1.htm
Find out how to stitch a pom-pom quilt, learn about collecting fountain pens, and discover what gives collections of Indian blankets their charm in this archive of articles from the magazine.

ANTIQUE ROADSHOW TIPS OF THE TRADE
http://www.pbs.org/wgbh/pages/roadshow/tips/index.html
The popular PBS show offers a library of getting-started articles on topics like how to tell electroplate silver from silver plating, "collecting for tomorrow," and how to spot ceramic defects.

PAMELA WIGGINS' GETTING STARTED ARTICLES
ON ABOUT.COM
http://antiques.about.com/hobbies/collecting/antiques
About.Com's intrepid guide to the world of antiques writes regular features on how to get started collecting. One of her topics of expertise is vintage apparel and accessories.

Looking for Good Reading About Antiques and Collectibles? You can read Ralph & Terry Kovel's syndicated column **Antiques & Collectibles on Hearst Corp.'s Homearts** Web site (**http://www.homearts.com**). Specifically, head to:
http://www.homearts.com/depts/home/kfkovef1.htm.
You'll find an archive of hundreds of past columns on topics as diverse as the collecting of soup tureens to the history of convertible beds. Or, head to **eBay's Collectibles Feature Library** (**http://pages.ebay.com/community/library**), where you'll find lots of great articles geared to getting you started collecting.

Free Help Figuring Out Antique and Collectible Terms

THE ANTIQUES GLOSSARY FROM ANTIQUERESOURCES.COM
http://www.antiqueresources.com/glossary/index.html
Look up the difference between an armoire and an astrolab in this extensive glossary of befuddling antique terms.

COLLECTOR'S UNIVERSE GLOSSARIES
http://www.collectorsuniverse.com
Collector's Universe offers big glossaries for dozens of different collecting interests including: advertising, Americana, ancient coins, antiques, art, autographs, banknotes, beanies, books, cigars, modern coins, comic books, cowboy memorabilia, cigars, dolls, diamonds, glass, gold, silver, golf collectibles, guitars, Indian collectibles, magazines, military, minerals, movie memorabilia, paper, photographs, porcelain, pottery, political collectibles, postcards, radio & TV collectibles, science-fiction collectibles, stamps, sports, surfing collectibles, toys, sports memorabilia, watches, trains, toys, and wine.

ABOUT ANTIQUE'S GLOSSARY
http://www.about-antiques.com/Glossary.htm
Learn the different between a butterfly table and a bat-wing in this extensive guide to antiquing terminology.

ANTIQUES WORLD'S INTRODUCTION TO ANTIQUES AND COLLECTIBLES
http://www.antiquesworld.com/reference/intro.html
What are antiques? What are collectibles? Yes, there is a difference.

"WHAT'S A WATERMARK?" BY RALPH & TERRY KOVEL
http://homearts.com/depts/home/kfkove68.htm

TOY TERMS FROM THE BIG RED TOYBOX
http://www.bigredtoybox.com/toyterms.htm

An "AM" is an "action man" and a "C1" is useful only for parts, while a "KF" has "kung-fu grip hands." If the acronyms in toy-related online discussion groups have you puzzled, look them up in this amazing glossary.

COMMON CIVIL WAR ACRONYMS, FROM ANTIQUERESOURCES.COM
http://www.antiqueresources.com/articles/cwacronyms.html

Did you know that AoC stands for "Army of the Cumberland" or that DUV are "Daughters of Union Veterans?" Antique Resources has compiled an extensive glossary of acronyms you might encounter while researching Civil War memorabilia.

LIZ COLLECTIBLES' "JEWELRY WORDS" GUIDE
http://www.lizjewel.com/words.htm

Click on "Jewelry Words" for definitions of phrases like "aurora borealis" and "florentine finish."

ANTIQUES WORLD DICTIONARY OF ANTIQUE AND ESTATE JEWELRY
http://www.antiquesworld.com/reference/jewelry.html

Discover what is meant by such terms as "art deco," "book chain" and "foilback."

ANTIQUES WORLD GUIDE TO PRECIOUS METAL AND GEMSTONE WEIGHTS & MEASURES
http://www.antiquesworld.com/reference/silvgold.html

KARIMA PARRY'S PLASTIC FANTASTIC GLOSSARY
http://www.plasticfantastic.com/glossary.html

Can't tell if it's bakelite or celluloid? Karima fills you in on the terms and on the colors used in different types of vintage plastic.

THE LANGUAGE OF DOLL COLLECTING
http://www.dollinfo.com/dollese.htm
Learn the subtleties of "dollese" by determining whether your doll has "applied ears" or is given to "sweating."

AUTOGRAPHING TERMS AND DEFINITIONS
http://www.autographcentral.com/getting_started/terms.html
Helpful terms to learn when discussing autographs.

ORIGINAL COMIC ART GLOSSARY
http://home.att.net/~ehodder/glossary.htm
An A-Z comic art glossary starting with "acid free" and ending with "zip-a-tone."

CYBERATTIC — PERIODS AND STYLES GLOSSARY
http://www.cyberattic.com/ref/periods.html
Wondering about the difference between middle- and late-Victorian? CyberAttic tells you which style is associated with which historical period.

 ## Free Help Dating Antiques and Collectibles

Properly dating an antique or collectible is an art. The best way to go about it is to join a discussion group and visit applicable Web sites—especially those by About.Com—for your type of collectible. Here are just a few Web sites on dating that we found to be fun and useful.

DETERMINING THE AGE OF ANTIQUE AND CLASSIC FISHING REELS
http://www.antiquefishingreels.com/
This site explains how to grade, value, and determine the age of your antique and classic fishing reels.

"A TRIP TO THE PATENT AND TRADEMARK OFFICE" BY MARY BELLIS

http://inventors.about.com/education/sciphys/
inventors/library/weekly/aa061499.htm

*Mary, the About.Com guide to Inventors
(**http://inventors.about.com**) tells you how to research patent
numbers.*

PATENT DATE CHART FROM ANTIQUES-SOUTHWEST.COM

http://www.antiques-southwest.com/patentchart.htm

*Look up the patent number on that toy or clock and find out the
year that it was issued.*

DATING YOUR SINGER SEWING MACHINE

http://users.erols.com/santilla/birthday/birthdate.htm

Krisi Santilla offers information to help you date your Singer.

DATING QUILTS—A BRIEF OVERVIEW

http://www.quilthistory.com/dating_quilts.htm

*Kris Driessen from Hickory Hill Antique Quilts
(**http://www.HickoryHillQuilts.com**) describes some of the fabrics,
colors, and styles used throughout history. Be sure to click on the
accompanying links for more information.*

40 YEARS WITH BARBIE

http://www.antiques-southwest.com/patentchart.htm

*Read about and view pictures of Barbie, from her introduction in
1959 through the present day.*

free Discussion Groups for Collectors

Discussing your collecting passion with other enthusiasts around the world is great fun. It's also the best way to learn how to care for your collectibles, the tricks of buying and selling them on the Internet, as well as in-person swap meets and flea-markets. There are many different types of discussion groups for collectors on the Web. These include:

• **E-mail or mailing list discussion groups.** To join you send an e-mail message to a computer. Messages from other group members are deposited in your e-mail box each day.

• **Bulletin boards.** You tap into a Web site and can read messages that other collectors post in different topics. You can respond to the messages either publicly or privately.

• **Newsgroups.** Newsgroups are public discussion groups whose messages swirl through cyberspace in a sort of bulletin-board-type free-for-all. To participate in newsgroup discussions you need to set up your Web browser or AOL's software to "subscribe" you to the newsgroup, then download any new messages whenever you log on to the Internet.

Mailing lists are often the most worthwhile—and lively—groups. Because of their semi-private nature, members freely share opinions on evaluating collectibles, shopping for them, and selling them.

Join a Discussion Group—We Can't Recommend It Strongly Enough! Internet discussion groups for collectors really are the best source of information available anywhere for learning how to care for, repair and sell your collectibles.

⬛ No Matter How Esoteric Your Collecting Passion, There is Probably a Discussion Group Out There Devoted to It

Whether you collect Legos or Zippo lighters, there is probably a discussion group for you. How can you find it? Head to the big general-interest collectible Web sites we recommend in Chapter 2, Free Big Web Sites About Antiques and Collectibles. Many offer guides to Web discussion groups for collectors. Here are more places to check:

• Head to **Collecting at About.Com** (**http://home.about.com/hobbies/collecting**) and tap your way into the special interest devoted to your species of collectible. The About.Com collectible guides offer wonderful, up-to-date lists of mailing lists for collectors.

• Also check out **The Internet Antique Shop** (**http://www.tias.com**), which hosts many mailing lists—and bulletin boards.

• Try searching some of the big mailing list directories like **The Liszt** (**http://www.liszt.com**) or **The List of Publicly Accessible Mailing Lists** (**http://www.neosoft.com/internet/paml**).

• Search the directories of Internet services that offer free mailing list hosting. A number of collectible discussion groups are run on **Onelist** (**http://www.onelist.com**). Also search **Dejanews Communities** (**http://www.dejanews.com**) and **eGroups** (**http://www.egroups.com**).

• Visit the Web sites of clubs devoted to your type of collectible. Also ask Web site owners who run large sites devoted to your collectible if they can recommend discussion groups.

✋ *Warning!* Do not sign up for mailing lists with "free e-mail" services like Juno, Hotmail, or Yahoo Mail. These lists generate lots of e-mail each day——so much mail that it will quickly fill up your mail box on these services and the mailing list will unsubscribe you. In fact, some mailing lists won't even permit people to subscribe who are using free e-mail services.

E-mail List Discussion Groups

Here is a selection of discussion lists for collectors. There are many, *many* more. If you don't see a group devoted to your collectible, follow our tips on previous pages to find a group for you.

ANTIQUE TALK
http://www.onelist.com
Antique Talk is about all kinds of antiques and collectibles.

THRILL OF THE HUNT
e-mail: Blu65ang@aol.com
A list devoted to antique and bargain hunting, concentrating on the Northeast, upstate New York, and New England. How to start an antique store is another a topic of discussion.

THE INTERNET ANTIQUE SHOP MAILING LISTS
http://www.tias.com
The Internet Antique Shop hosts a number of excellent mailing lists, including ones devoted to these subjects: antique jewelry; art glass; art pottery; arts and crafts; buttons; fine china porcelain; furniture; marbles; Royal Doulton; vintage accessories; and watches. They also host bulletin boards for many of these mailing lists to supplement discussions. To join the lists, head to TIAS's main page and click "Resources." Scroll down the page to the Mailing List section. To read the bulletin boards, click "Bulletin Boards."

PEACE LIST DISCUSSION GROUPS
http://www.peacelist.com
This service runs mailing lists devoted to coins, cars, books, dolls, art, jewels, music, pottery, ephemera, porcelain, glass, stamps, trading cards, Beanies, and other toys.

THE VINTAGE CLOTHING LIST
Write to majordomo@indra.com
with this in the message: subscribe vintage
Discuss vintage clothing—where to buy it, how to preserve it, how to sell it—with other vintage fans.

VINTAGE ACCESSORIES
http://www.onr.com/user/pam/listserve.html
A discussion group devoted to purses, gloves, hats, and other accessories.

LIZ BRYMAN'S JEWELCOLLECT
http://www.lizjewel.com/jc.html
Discuss collecting, repairing, buying, and selling vintage costume jewelry.

JEWELRYTALK
http://www.gemsplusonline.com/JewelryTalk.htm
Another e-mail list devoted to discussing vintage costume jewelry. You'll also find chat rooms and bulletin boards at the group's Web site.

ABOUT.COM'S GUIDE TO ACTION FIGURE MAILING LISTS
http://actionfigures.about.com/hobbies/collecting/actionfigures/msub41.htm
or
http://actionfigures.about.com
Learn how to sign up for the many Internet discussion groups for toy collectors. There's even a list for collectors of bootleg toys.

Look for the Mailing List's FAQ for Answers to Your Collectible Questions Many mailing lists maintain FAQs or resource lists of good ideas, book reviews, and collecting hints compiled by members. Check the mailing list's Web page or ask other members of the list if a FAQ exists.

One such list is **The JewelCollect Resource List** by Marcelle (Belle) Higginbotham (**http://members. tripod.lycos.com/~asiteforme/JCResourceList.html**). It includes a directory of links to vintage jewelry books, videos, and information around the Web.

THE HISTORY OF PHOTOGRAPHY MAILING LIST
http://palimpsest.stanford.edu/byform/mailing-lists/
photohstsearch.html

THE OLD TOOLS E-MAIL DISCUSSION GROUP
You can read an archive of past messages at:
http://mailmunch.law.cornell.edu/mhonarc/OLDTOOLS//thrd50.html

You can read the group's FAQ at:
http://www.mcs.net/~brendler/oldtools/OTFAQ.htm

To join the list send an e-mail to: listserv@listserv.law.cornell.edu
In the message type:
subscribe oldtoolsYourFullName

THE VASELINE GLASS E-MAIL DISCUSSION GROUP
http://www.southern-belle.com/vaselinelist.shtml

EARLY AMERICAN PATTERN GLASS DISCUSSION GROUP
http://www.ritzcom.net/wheatina/EAPGlass/discuss.htm

THE GOOFUS GLASS E-MAIL DISCUSSION GROUP
http://sundial.net/~gballens

MAPTRADE MAILING LIST (FOR ANTIQUE MAP COLLECTORS)
http://www.raremaps.com/maptrade

POSTCARD LIST
http://ourworld.compuserve.com/homepages/lcseiler/instr.htm

THE INTERNET POSTCARD & COLLECTING CLUB LIST
http://www.web-pac.com/mall/club/clubform.html

ANTIQUE BOTTLES
To subscribe, e-mail listserv@home.ease.lsoft.com.
In the message, type: subscribe antique-bottle yourfullname

ANTIQUE TELEPHONE COLLECTORS
To subscribe, e-mail listserv@maelstrom.stjohns.edu
In the message, type: subscribe atca

Collectible Mailing Lists Are Fun and Informative, but You Need to Follow the Rules

No matter what your interests, mailing lists are your best source of information on the Internet. But before you sign up for one, you should read its rules for joining and posting to the list. Then, follow our tips on mailing list netiquette.

• **When you join a mailing list, the computer that runs the list will automatically mail you directions for participating. Print them, keep them near at hand.** Take note of the list's different e-mail addresses. You will be sending mail to one address, and sending any subscription changes to a different "administrative" address. *Don't send messages to subscribe or unsubscribe to the list to the main address. That will broadcast your message to everyone on the list!*

• **Collectible lists have rules about whether or not you can post messages about items you have for sale.** Some lists encourage members to post messages about items they have for sale on eBay or elsewhere. Other lists forbid it. Some lists maintain bulletin boards for members to post sale notices. Be sure to find out your list's nettiquette. *And please don't try to circumvent the rules by posting messages that pertain to a topic under discussion and ending the message with "By the way, I have yadda-yadda for sale on eBay today!"*

• **You probably have only a limited amount of disk space on your ISP to store incoming e-mail. That means that if you're a member of a mailing list that generates lots of mail, the mail may overrun your mailbox if you don't check your e-mail daily.** When that happens, e-mail that people send you will bounce back to them. And the list may automatically unsubscribe you because messages are bouncing back. The solution: subscribe to the digest version of the list, if one is available, and unsubscribe from the list if you're going out of town.

• **If the mailing list has rules about how mail to the list should be addressed, follow them.** Many lists request that members include the list's name in the **Subject:** line of any messages so that members who have set up their e-mail software to filter messages can do so effectively. You should also try to make the **Subject:** line of your message as informative as possible for readers who don't have time to read every message posted to the list.

• **Never include your address, phone number or other personal information in a mailing list post.** Many mailing lists are archived—which means that everyone on the Internet might be able to read them until the end of time!

• **If the mailing list has an archive of past messages or a frequently asked questions file, check them before posting your question to the list, since someone may have already answered it.**

• **Never send an e-mail attachment of a picture to a list unless this sort of thing is permitted.**

• **When replying to a message, before you hit the Send button, take a look at the message's address to check where it's going.** Don't send a personal reply to everyone on the mailing list. And don't hit Reply to All if the message is addressed to many different people or lists.

Here are a few mailing list terms you might encounter:

Moderated List—All messages that are mailed to the list are first sent to a moderator to screen before being broadcast to everyone on the list. No, it's not censorship, but merely a tactic to keep messages to the topic under discussion and, on some lists, to prevent "flame wars" from breaking out between disagreeing members.

Unmoderated List—Messages are not screened.

Digest—Messages are collected into one long e-mail message that is sent at the end of the day to members who subscribe to the list's "digest version."

Archive—Some mailing list messages are stored in vast libraries on a Web site for others to search and read years later.

FAQ—Most lists have a "frequently asked question" file that contains questions to answers that list members commonly ask. Usually the FAQ is stored on the list's Web site, although some lists allow members to retrieve the file through e-mail.

Newsgroups

There are many Usenet newsgroups devoted to many different kinds of collectibles. Newsgroups tend to be less "clubby" than mailing lists. Some are pretty raucous because there's no one moderating the discussion. Still, they are valuable sources of information for collectors. Head to Chapter 1 for directions on how to subscribe to them and read messages through your ISP or AOL. Here are just a few of the many newsgroups about collectibles. (As you can see, we haven't even begun to list the ones devoted to *Star Trek* collectibles!) For a complete list of collectibles-related newsgroups, head to **Antique.Org's Newsgroup Page (http://www.Antique.org/antiquenewsgroups.html)**.

Head to Chapter 1 for directions on how to download and read newsgroups with your browse or through AOL.

Warning to Parents! The Usenet newsgroups are unmoderated and uncensored. We spotted a lot of pornography in some of the collectors newsgroups, particularly ones for children's collectibles.

> **rec.antiques**
> **rec.antiques.bottles**
> **rec.antiques.marketplace**
> **rec.antiques.radio+phone**
> **alt.collecting**
> **alt.collecting.8-track-tapes**
> **alt.collecting.autographs**
> **alt.collecting.barbie**
> **alt.collecting.beanie-babies**
> **alt.collecting.beanie-babies.discussion.moderated**
> **alt.collecting.beanie-babies.forsale**
> **alt.collecting.beanie-babies.tradingcards**
> **alt.collecting.beanie-babies.uk**
> **alt.collecting.bicycles**
> **alt.collecting.breweriana**
> **alt.collecting.casino-tokens**
> **alt.collecting.pens-pencils**
> **alt.collecting.postcard**
> **alt.collecting.records**
> **alt.collecting.sports-figures**

alt.collecting.stamps
alt.collecting.stamps.us
alt.collecting.stamps.worldwide
alt.collecting.teddy-bears
alt.collecting.toy-robot
alt.collecting.warner-bros
alt.disney.collecting
alt.fan.stamp.collecting
alt.fan.plushies
alt.marketplace.collectables
alt.military.collecting
alt.military.collecting.medals
alt.rec.collecting.stamps.discuss
alt.rec.collecting.stamps.marketplace
alt.toys
rec.arts.sf.starwars.collecting.customizing
rec.arts.sf.starwars.collecting.misc
rec.arts.sf.starwars.collecting.vintage
rec.collecting
rec.collecting.books
rec.collecting.cards.discuss
rec.collecting.cards.non-sports
rec.collecting.coins
rec.collecting.dolls
rec.collecting.paper-money
rec.collecting.pins
rec.collecting.postal-history
rec.collecting.sport.baseball
rec.collecting.sport.basketball
rec.collecting.sport.football
rec.collecting.sport.hockey
rec.collecting.sport.misc
rec.collecting.stamps.discuss
rec.collecting.stamps.marketplace
rec.collecting.villages
rec.music.collecting.misc
rec.music.collecting.vinyl
rec.toys.lego
rec.toys.vintage
rec.toys.cars
rec.toys.action-figures
rec.toys.gijoe.1980s
rec.toys.misc

Read Newsgroups Through Dejanews Would you like to browse through a few newsgroups, but are feeling too lazy to set up your browser to subscribe to them and download messages from your ISP? Head to Dejanews (**http://www.dejanews.com**) to read newsgroups. You can also use Dejanews' search feature to search archives of past messages for ones pertaining to your favorite collectible. Some of Dejanews' message archives stretch back to the early days of the Internet.

In order to participate in chats on collectible Web sites, you need to be running an up-to-date browser with Java enabled. In **Netscape**, pull down the **Edit** menu and select **Preferences**. Click **Advanced**. Place checks beside **Enable Java** and **Enable Javascript**. Click **OK**. In **Explorer**, from the Tools menu, select **Internet Options**. Click the **Security** tab. Click the **Internet** icon. Under **Java Permissions**, select "High Safety." Under **Scripting/Active Scripting**, select "Enable." Under **Scripting of Java Applets**, select "Enable." Click **OK** when you're done.

Read About the History of Sports and Finance Head to the **Museum of American Financial History** (**http://www.mafh.org**) to read articles from the museum's magazine on topicps like "How American Investored Financed the Early Growth of Baseball." And to learn about the history of golf equipment, head to Old Course (**http://www.oldcourse.com**).

Bulletin Boards

To read bulletin board messages, all you need to do is point
your Web browser toward the discussion's URL and jump in.
You can find many bulletin boards for collectors at the **Internet
Antique Shop** (**http://www.tias.com**; click "Bulletin Boards").
You'll also find some in the different collectible forums at
About.Com (**http:// home.about.com/hobbies/collecting**). Here
are a few more that we found interesting.

*You'll find message boards in over 75 collectible categories from Armani and
Art Deco to Wedgwood, from wizards to dragons at World Collectors.*

WORLD COLLECTORS NET MESSAGE BOARD AND CHAT ROOMS
http://www.worldcollectorsnet.com/boards.html

THE INTERNET ANTIQUE STORE VINTAGE CLOTHING & ACCESSORIES BULLETIN BOARD
http://www.tias.com/ubb/Forum131/HTML/000006.html

ZELDA'S VINTAGE CLOTHING BOARD
http://www.antiquemalls.com/cgi-bin/UltraBoard/UltraBoard.cgi

THE GLASS MUSEUM'S GLASS CLUB BULLETIN BOARD
http://www.glass.co.nz/bulletinboard.html

THE JUKEBOX COLLECTOR BULLETIN BOARD
http://www.juke-index.co.nz

SPRATLING SILVER COLLECTING BULLETIN BOARD
http://www.spratlingsilver.com

The most active message board at The Collector's Coffee Shop is "What is this and what is it worth?"

THE COLLECTOR'S COFFEE SHOP
http://collectorpages.com/forums.html

ANTIQUE WEEK COMMUNITY
http://www.antiqueweek.com/comm/awcomm.htm

COMPOSITION DOLL BULLETIN BOARD
http://www.wwvisions.com/craftbb/composition.html

TY TALK CYBERBOARD
http://www.ty.com/cyberboard/index.html
The Official Beanie Baby Board.

EVERYTHING FURBY INTERACTIVE MESSAGE BOARD
http://www.corban-consulting.com/furby/bb4/wwwbd4.htm

FURNITURE WIZARD DISCUSSION BOARD
http://www.furniturewizard.com/wwwboard/wwwboard.html

KEN HITCHCOCK'S AUTOGRAPH REFERENCE LIBRARY BULLETIN BOARD
http://www.x-pointcgi.com/cgi-bin/users/5686/wwwboard/wwwboard.html

ALADDIN LIGHTS BULLETIN BOARD
http://www.aladdinknights.org/bboard

 Web Rings

A "web ring" is a group of Web sites that have linked to each other for the convenience of surfers who like to click from one related site to another. Most collectible-themed Web rings are collections of shopping sites. Some, like the History Ring, consist of Web pages of enthusiasts.

In order to travel a web ring you don't need to "join" it. You merely click from one page to another through the Web ring's logo. Some rings have a "list sites" link that allows you to view links and descriptions to all the participating sites. Web rings can take you to illuminating and revelatory Web pages, regardless of whether you're shopping or not.

ANTIQUE RING
http://www.Antique.org/antiquering.html

ANTIQUES, POSTCARDS, AND COLLECTIBLES WEBRING
http://www.web-pac.com/mall/webpacring

Antiques, Postcard & Collectibles WebRing

Prev | Skip | Next 5 | Random | Next
Web-Pac Antiques, Postcards
& Collectibles WebRing Member Listing

BEST ANTIQUE & COLLECTIBLES SITES
http://computrends.com/antiquering.html

THE BOTTLE COLLECTOR'S WEB RING
http://members.tripod.com/~AlanCheshire/botring.html

THE ANTIQUE LIGHTING WEB RING
http://www.rushlight.org/webring.html

THE COLLECTIBLE COSTUME JEWELRY WEB RING
http://www.fix.net/~grdnprty/webring.html

THE JEWELRY WEB RING
http://www.htcomp.net/website/ring.html

THE ART GLASS WEB RING
http://www.southern-belle.com/webring.shtml

THE HISTORY RING
http://members.tripod.com/~PHILKON/ring.html

NASSAU STREET WEB RING (STAMP COLLECTORS)
http://www.stampauctions.com/ring

STAMP DEALERS WEB RING
http://www.stampdealers.com

ANTIQUE AMMUNITION WEBRING
http://members.tripod.com/rrbar/webring.html

ANTIQUE DOLL WEB RING
http://members.aol.com/VintajBebe/ring/antiqd.html

ANTIQUE AUTOMOBILE WEB RING
http://www.aaca.org/webring

CAT COLLECTIBLES WEB RING
http://www.teleport.com/~tyberk/CCWR.html

THE PHONOGRAPH RING
http://php.indiana.edu/~pfeaster/phono.htm

CARNIVAL GLASS WEB RING
http://carnival.ksnews.com/carnivalglass

DIECAST COLLECTIBLES WEB RING
http://www.diecastmall.net/ring.html

GI JOE COLLECTORS WEB RING
http://pages.prodigy.com/ttlic/gi_joe.htm

ANTIQUE WEBRING
http://www.eANTIQUE.org/webring.html

FROM ANOTHER TIME WEB RING
http://anothertime.com/TheMall/WebRing.htm

ANTIQUES, ARTGLASS, AND COLLECTIBLES
http://www.southern-belle.com/webring.shtml

BARBIE COLLECTORS RING
http://www.srhein.simplenet.com/dolldoctor2.html#Collector Ring

free Web Auctions— and Free Advice on How to Spot Bargains

Don't you wish you could wander fleamarkets every day, poking through cigar boxes of old ribbons, examining lamps? Web auctions like eBay are just like fleamarkets, and therein lays their appeal. You tap into the auction site with your browser and sift through thousands of items—the sorts of things you'd find at a garage sale, from half-completed needle-point kits to old car parts. Amid the junk there are always bargains. Whether you collect Barbies or baseballs, chances are you'll spot enough goodies to keep you tapping into the auction site day after day.

How Web Auctions Work

First you need to register on the auction site—usually provide just your name and address. When you bid on an item, you specify the maximum amount you're willing to pay. The auction site automatically ups your bid by small increments of, say, a dollar as others bids. If you're outbid, the auction site e-mails you—in case you want to bid again. An auction can run from one day to several weeks. An auction can also have a "reserve price" which means that if bidding doesn't meet a set, usually undisclosed price, the seller doesn't have to sell it to the highest bidder.

If you're the winning bidder, the auction site e-mails you. You need to contact the item's seller and work out a payment arrangement. In most cases the auction site is not involved in the transaction. If you don't get the item, or if it's defective and the seller won't give you your money back, your only recourse

Read News About the Online Auction World
At AuctionWatch (**http://www.auctionwatch.com**) you can read news, reviews and gossip about the world of online auctions.

An increasing number of Web sites let you search and monitor auctions on multiple auction sites at once. One such service is **AuctionRover** (**http://www.auctionrover.com**). Search for "rhinestone watch" and AuctionRover will search multiple auction sites like Amazon and eBay looking for items.

Other similar services include **E-compare** (**http://www.ecompare.com/index-auction.html**) and **Bidder's Edge** (**http://www.biddersedge.com**). Tell iTrack (**http://www.itrack.com/**) to search auction sites for a particular item and the service will e-mail you when the item is up for bid. The disadvantage of these services is that they can be bedeviling to use. Also, some Web auction sites forbid these services' "robots" from searching their listings.

© The Collectibles Exchange

The Collectibles Exchange is an auction-like system, just for Beanies (**http://www.beaniex.com**). *You tell the Exchange which Beanies you have that you wish to trade. You tell the Exchange which Beanies you want to buy. The Exchange serves as a middle-man to the sale, telling you how much you can get for your Beanie from other waiting buyers, and how much you will pay for the Beanies you want. Then it tabulates your order. Keep in mind that it's going to pay you only wholesale prices for your Beanie. The Exchange also authenticates Beanies and will only broker ones in pristine condition. No crumpled hang-tags, please!*

The Big Web Auctions for Collectibles

EBAY
http://www.ebay.com

YAHOO AUCTIONS
http://auctions.yahoo.com

AMAZON.COM AUCTIONS
http://auctions.amazon.com

 # Smaller Web Auctions with Lots of Collectibles

FAIRMARKET
http://www.fairmarket.com

AUCTION UNIVERSE
http://www.auctionuniverse.com

COLLECTORS UNIVERSE
http://collectors.com/auctions

Collectors Universe is a good place to go for auctions of sports collectibles, although the site hosts auctions in many different collectibles categories.

uAuction is a smaller Web auction site with a focus on antiques and collectibles.

BOXLOT
http://www.boxlot.com

UAUCTION
http://www.uauction.com

UP4SALE
http://www.up4sale.com

GOLD'S AUCTION
http://www.goldsauction.com/apps/index.html

SWAPPERS AND COLLECTORS
http://swappersandcollectors.com

COLLECTING NATION
http://www.collectingnation.com

EHAMMER AUCTIONS
http://www.ehammer.com

◐ What About "Live" Auctions on the Internet?

If you'd love to attend an auction at a ritzy auction house in New York or Zurich but fear that with your six-inch stilettos and rhinestone jacket you might not get in the door, consider tapping into a cybercast auction. "Live" auction Web sites like **Amazon.Com's Livebid (http://www.livebid.com)** and **The Auction Channel (http://www.theauctionchannel.com)** let you experience the thrill of the gavel through your Web browser. Dozens of auction houses around the world broadcast their live auctions over the Web, auctioning off everything from boxing memorabilia to perfume bottles and real estate. You can bid online, or over the phone, assuming that you've registered in advance.

On Livebid, you can listen to the auctioneer while pictures of items up for auction flash on your screen, along with the bids. To tap in, you need the free browser plugin **RealAudio** or **RealPlayer (http://www.real.com)**, an up-to-date browser, and a PC with a Pentium II or better processor or a PowerMac G3 or better.

At The Auction Channel, you don't need anything fancy to tap in, except for an up-to-date Web browser with Java and Javascript enabled.

While The Auction Channel offers a "grandstand" feature that lets you watch the bidding without registering to bid, in general you need to complete a fairly lengthy registration process in advance of the auction in order to watch, just as you would at an in-person auction. You might need to supply information like your driver's license, work phone, and credit card numbers. In exchange you get a password or PIN. But it's up to the auction house to decide whether to give you a "cyber seat" in the auction. The servers that run these services have finite capacity, so the auction houses like to ensure that the bidders-with-bucks can tap in. They might also want to discourage nosey 12-year-olds from hogging the bandwidth.

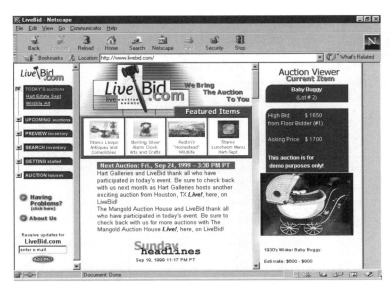

On Amazon.Com's Livebid you can listen to the auctioneer as prices and pictures roll over your screen.

The Auction Channel hosts cyber auctions by dozens of well-known auction houses. You can bid on everything from castles on the Rhine to wicker lounges.

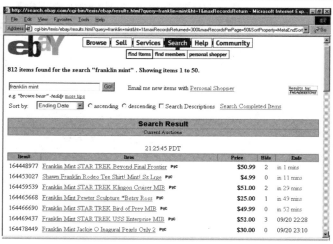

It's Franklin Mint Mania on eBay! If you've always wanted a Klingon Bird of Prey or string of Jackie-O pearls, head to the auction site and search for "franklin mint." You'll find auctions for nearly a thousand items.

You Can Buy Excess Factory Inventory of Some Collectible Lines on Auction Sites

Many dealers on eBay and other auction sites sell excess factory inventory of well-known collectibles. For instance, you'll find a lot of Franklin Mint collectibles selling on eBay for a fraction of the price Franklin Mint originally sold them through magazine ads. You can also find merchandise from many (although not all) cable shopping-show collectibles lines, like Joan Rivers jewelry, selling on eBay. If you collect these things you can snare some *terrific buys*. (Use the auction site's search feature to search for **franklin mint, joan rivers,** or whatever.)

But there are a few precautions to keep in mind. Sometimes you're bidding on manufacturing seconds, but the dealers may not admit this—or they may not even know, because they bought the items from a third-party liquidator. If you ask them if you're bidding on a factory second, they may merely reply, "It's new and in the original box." Make sure the dealer has a return policy. (Factory seconds are not necessarily bent and mangled. Judy used to work in a factory and, when her eyes got bleary, would pull off the line and toss into the reject bin anything that didn't catch the light just right. She would not be surprised if other factory rejecters are similarly capricious.)

Also, sometimes you can't be sure that an item up for auction really is a bona fide member of the line of collectibles that you seek. The item might not be marked, the dealer might have purchased it from someone who told them it was part of a particular line when it's not, and so on.

Tap Into Sotheby Auctions on Amazon.Com

You can't watch those famous Sotheby auctions live on the Net (at least not yet). But you can bid on special Sotheby auctions cyber-fleamarket-style on Amazon.Com's auction site (**http://sothebys.amazon.com**). The advantage of these auctions over commonplace cyber-fleamarkets like eBay is that you get the Sotheby's guarantee of authenticity on items. Bogus imposters of just-about-everything are rampant in cyber-fleamarkets. If you're buying pricey collectibles, especially ones like autographed sports memorabilia that can be hard to authenticate, the Sotheby's guarantee is worthwhile.

JUDY & GLORIA'S TIPS FOR PARTICIPATING IN "LIVE" WEB AUCTIONS

• If you plan to bid, preview items before the auction. Write down auction numbers and details and contact the auction house directly with any questions.

• If the auction site offers a simulator, practice bidding before the event.

• If you're going to be bidding on high-ticket items, you should research the auction house in advance by talking to other collectors.

• Keep in mind during the auction that prices that appear on the auction site may not be keeping up with what's happening at the auction house.

• Be patient. Sometimes the pictures on the Web site don't match up with what's up for auction.

• If the auctioneer's voice sounds garbled or the auction Web site looks slow, it may be due to high Internet traffic or because many bidders are accessing the site. There's nothing you can do but be patient.

• Auction houses post the winning bids within a week or so after the auction. If you're not sure at the end of the auction whether you got the winning bid, the best thing to do is to wait for the auction house to contact you, or check the postings.

See Chapter 11 for our tips on listening to Webcasts with RealPlayer and RealAudio.

Judy & Gloria's Survival Guide for Buying Stuff in Cyber-Fleamarkets

We love to shop. And we know that you do too. But just like clawing your way through a sale table in Ladies Lingerie, the disorderly world of cyber-fleamarkets demands that you play street tough. We're not talking live auctions simulcast on the Web, but rather fleamarket-style auctions like eBay: ones where you bid one day and hope that you win a week later. Here are our tips.

Tips for Selecting Items on Which to Bid

Safety in buying stuff from Web auctions depends upon what you're buying. High-ticket items are high risk. High-ticket items like autographs that you can't authenticate simply by ogling a fuzzy scan on your computer screen are even higher risk. Remember that in most cases you're not actually buying from the auction site but from an individual whom you know nothing about except for his or her e-mail address. Judy often buys vintage sewing supplies, accessories, and grandma beads from sellers on eBay. She has yet to get fleeced, but she rarely buys anything over $50. She would never buy a $30K Victorian highboy from a stranger on eBay.

Bid on auction Web sites that offer some kind of money-back guarantee. A few of the auction sites offer compensation if you get fleeced. Ebay offers up to $200 on auctions in which the final bid is over $25. Amazon.Com offers up to $250, but only on auctions that carry the Amazon Auction Guarantee logo—be sure to look for that logo before you bid!

Learn as much as you can about what you're buying. Being knowledgeable about the sorts of things you collect is your best defense against being sold something that's not what it's described as being. This is as true in cyber-fleamarkets as it is in in-person ones. Learn how to distinguish manufacturers' or craftsman's marks. Learn the distinguishing qualities of the item you're collecting. Learn how to spot imposters. Chit-chat with other collectors through the mailing lists and discussion

Look for the Amazon Guarantee logo on auctions you bid on Amazon.Com. That doesn't guarantee that the item you're bidding on is authentic, but rather that you'll get your money back if you get taken —and the amount is under $250.

groups we recommend in Chapter 4 because other collectors are the best source of knowledge and tips.

Don't believe everything you read in descriptions. One seller's "mint condition" may be your "shabby chic," especially when it comes to antiques. One seller's "Victorian" hat box may be K-Mart in disguise. While some fleamarket sellers tiptoe the line between poetic license and outright fraud, most are simply ignorant of what they're selling. Face it, we all can't be experts on Edwardian jabots. Here are some phrases you should read skeptically:

- *"I think it's [insert name of favorite metal, gem, historical period], but I could be wrong."* Judy once bought on eBay a necklace described as "It came in a plastic bag marked 'silver' and I think it's turquoise. I think it's American Indian from the '40s." It turned out to be a glass necklace of unidentifiable metal from the Victorian era. Luckily, she didn't pay much and she's not fussy.

- *"This came from the estate of [insert name of favorite deceased movie star]. I don't have a certificate of authenticity, but a woman I trust very much bought it from the estate and swears that's where she got it."*

- *"This is from my grandmother's estate. She was 92 when she died, so it must be very old."* This commonly spotted eBay descriptive assumes that Grandma didn't buy anything in the second half of her life.

- "Deco-like," "Victorian-like," "Edwardian-like" and so on. Just because something is "like" stuff in a particular historical era doesn't mean it's from that era. Our favorite is "Titanic-like." Does that mean it will sink?

Ask what the item is made of, its dimensions, and how substantial it is. Don't assume that the translucent bust of Napolean is crystal. Don't assume that the old fashioned store sign is wooden. Don't even assume that the frying pan is iron. For that matter, don't assume that the silver spoons are not paper thin. One eBayite got burned when the supposed "authentic antique sign from Coney Island" she paid hundreds of dollars for turned out to be lightweight polyurethane foam. Ask lots of questions about the item's size, weight, and composition before you bid.

If you doubt the authenticity of an item, ask the seller how they know it's so. For instance, if an item is advertised as "gold," ask the seller if it's stamped with any karat or gold hallmark. If it's not ask them if they've tested the metal, and if so, how. If an item is sold as a name-brand ceramic or porcelain ask to see a scan of the maker's hallmark.

Hire a third-party appraiser or authentication service for high-ticket collectibles. Or check out the Sotheby's auctions on Amazon.Com. For pricey items like sports collectibles, autographs, coins, high-end antiques, or Beanies, consider hiring an appraiser or a certification or authentication service. Head to Chapter 6 for tips on finding these services and learning more about them. You can also head to eBay's primer on these services (**http://pages.ebay.com/services/safeharbor/safe harbor-auth-overview.html**). Sotheby's also offers authentication in conjunction with the special auctions they hold on Amazon.Com (**http://sothebys.amazon.com**).

Never assume anything about an item's condition. Something that looks great in a jpeg on Yahoo may arrive in your mailbox demanding to be fumigated. Ask specifics about the item's state: If it's fabric, does it smell? If it has rhinestones, are they cloudy? If it's glass, are there any chips or hairline cracks? Does the garment have any tears, moth holes, or worn spots? Does the doll have all its hair?

Be sure to ask too whether the item has ever been restored or repaired in any way. That's something that dealers often neglect to mention in descriptions.

Sellers sometimes say in their description that an item has been appraised at some rather outlandish dollar amount. This is usually meaningless unless the item has been appraised by a certified appraiser or valuator of some repute.

Tips for Selecting People to Buy From

Before you bid, check the seller's buyer ratings. Web auction sites let buyers post comments about sellers after a transaction. Although these "buyer ratings" are often not what they're cracked up to be—they can be easily forged— and aggrieved buyers may be too timid to post 'negative feedback', if a seller boasts hundreds of happy customers that can be a good sign that they will in fact send you your 99 cent buttons without laundering your check.

Avoid sellers who keep their feedback private. Some services let sellers make bad feedback invisible.

Buy from sellers with a return policy. Some sellers sell items "as is" and "no returns." This is not a good sign.

Look at the seller's other auctions. Some dealers sell only one type of collectible, like watches or toys. Sometimes you can get a sense from their other auctions whether they're experienced selling these types of items and whether their descriptions are accurate. Sometimes too you can get a sense whether they're given to describing items with tacky come-on phrases and over-inflated claims.

Find out before you bid what the seller plans to charge for shipping and whether they will ship the item insured. Amazingly, some sellers don't want to bother insuring items.

Avoid sellers who will accept only money orders. If you send a money order you have no way of knowing that your money actually arrived in their hands and they cashed the check.

Avoid sellers who will not agree to use an escrow service. An escrow service acts as a middle-man in the transaction. You mail the check to the escrow service. The seller sends you the item. When you inform the service that you've received the item satisfactorily, the service forwards your check on to the seller. Some online auction sites offer this service for a modest fee. If you're buying a pricey item you should ask the seller before you bid whether they'll use an escrow service. Two popular ones are iEscrow (**http://www.iescrow.com**) and TradeSafe (**http://www.tradesafe.com**).

Avoid sellers who use free e-mail services. These include Yahoo, Hotmail, Excite, and Bigfoot. These e-mail addresses are untraceable. While some sellers who use e-mail addresses on these services may be reputable, free e-mail services make it too easy for fraudulent sellers to hop from one untraceable address to another.

Avoid sellers with bizarro e-mail handles. If someone answers your e-mail with some weird e-mail name or address like "Prince of Darkness," shop elsewhere. Listen to your gut. If you have any reservations at all about doing business with someone, don't bid. Reputable sellers will verify their identity.

Do not buy from anyone who e-mails you after you have lost an auction. They may say, "I noticed you bid on such-and-such. I have some extra inventory. Would you like to buy it?" In these cases they were using the auction as a come-on.

For high-ticket items, select sellers who will let you pay with a credit card. There are advantages to paying by credit card. If you never receive the item or if the item is defective, you can complain to the credit card money and get your money back.

Be skeptical of sellers who claim to be auctioning items off for a charity. Charity scams abound on Web auction sites. A good tip-off of a scam is that the name of the charity isn't specified or sounds rather vague.

Join online collectors clubs whose members buy from each other. There are several mailing lists devoted to specific sorts of collectibles in which members agree to subscribe to a code of ethics when selling items. Although there is no way for these groups to enforce their codes of ethics, they're still worthwhile to join, since members are at least committed to good behavior. One such group is **Liz Bryman's Jewelcollect (http://www.lizjewel.com/jc.html)** for vintage jewelry lovers.

Web Auctions Graphics Tip! When your browser is downloading a picture of an item up for bid on a Web auction site it's actually downloading the picture from the Internet service of the seller—or in some cases, a free image hosting site. It's not getting it from the auction site. If the picture is slow to appear or doesn't display properly it's usually the fault of the service where the seller has posted their photos. If you don't see the picture, right-click (or click-hold on a Mac) on the "broken" image or the fractured image icon. From the pop-up box select **View Image**. This will sometimes reload just the picture.

Tips for Bargain Hunting

Check the "Ending Today" listings for the best buys. Most people bid on items in the last hours—or even the last minute—before an auction ends. (People who bid in the last minute are called "snipers.")

Check back every day. So many thousands of items are added to the big auction sites each day—some auctions run for only 24 hours—that it's a good strategy to check regularly.

Use the auction site's global search engine if you're shopping for something specific. If you're looking for something particular, like poodle-themed embroidery patterns from the '50s, search the entire auction site for different words, combinations of words, shortened forms of words, and even misspellings. For instance—poodle, podle, emb., poodle pat.—will all turn up patterns with the proper qualifications. We've found quilt tops accidentally posted with the Rolex watches this way.

Use the auction's watch list feature to inform you of new items. Some auction sites like **Microsoft**'s (**http://auctions.msn.com/scripts/agentmain.asp**) offer a watch list or "agent" feature that will inform you by e-mail of auctions in your area of interest.

Look at auctions that end at odd times. Most sellers set up their auctions to end during times when lots of people are logged on, like in the evening. That's when last-minute bidding is most apt to heat up. If you look at auctions that end late at night or during the day, the likelihood of someone outbidding you is less.

Check out auction items that appear to be clumsily described. That "chunk of glass, might be a paperweight" could be pricey Swarovski crystal. That "old yellow glass necklace" could be early 19th century Czech beads. Not everyone is as savvy about your favorite collectible as you are.

Check auction categories where your collectible might have been posted erroneously. For instance, check the "primitive art" category as well as the "textile" and "crafts" ones if you're searching for old needlepoint canvases.

Tips on What to Do If You Get Fleeced

Where do you go if the "Victorian shaving mug" looks like it came from Wal-mart and the seller has stopped answering your e-mail? The first thing to do is to promptly report it to the Web auction site.

Ebay offers up to $200 compensation on auctions in which the final bid is over $25. But the service must receive a complaint within 30 days after the auction's close. Amazon.Com offers up to $250 compensation, but only on auctions that carry the Amazon Auction Guarantee logo.

Beyond this minimal insurance, the auction sites tend not to get involved in auctions-gone-awry, unless the seller is a repeat offender.

If the money involved is significant there's a chance you might get law enforcement officials interested in helping you, but don't count on that either. Since Web auctions involve money mailed or transferred across state lines, contact postal officials, your local U.S. attorney's office, and the Federal Trade Commission. Be a pest, and call as many times as you need to get someone's attention.

This is why your best defense is to carefully choose what you bid on, and who you buy from.

You can read more consumer tips about Web auctions, and Internet shopping in general at these consumer protection Web sites:

NATIONAL FRAUD INFORMATION CENTER (INTERNET FRAUD WATCH)
http://www.fraud.org

NATIONAL CONSUMERS LEAGUE
http://www.natlconsumersleague.org

THE BETTER BUSINESS BUREAU ONLINE
http:/www.bbb.org

THE FEDERAL TRADE COMMISSION
http://www.ftc.gov/ftc/consumer.htm
http://www.ftc.gov

NEW YORK STATE ATTORNEY GENERAL'S INTERNET CONSUMER TIPS
http://www.oag.state.ny.us/consumer/consumer_issues.html

free Help Figuring Out What It's Worth

It's called the *Antiques Roadshow* phenomenon, after the popular PBS show in which ordinary people learn that their ordinary junk may be worth beacoup bucks. Now everyone suspects that there is a box in their attic harboring a collectible or two that, when sold at Sotheby's, will pay off their mortgage. (What most TV viewers don't realize about *Roadshow* is that appraisers on the show spend long days during filming sifting through junk that is indeed junk, and informing aspiring collectible tycoons that the junk they've carted in to be appraised is, well, junk.)

If you tap into the Internet hoping to learn the value of that tangled nest of toy trains or Grandma's broach, what you need to know is that the very worst thing you can do is tap into a collectibles mailing list or discussion group and announce, "I've got an 1884 such-and-such. Can someone tell me what it's worth?" Most likely no one will be able to tell you what it's worth. Worse, you will have breached the most sacrosanct rule of Internet collectible nettiquette. *No one can tell you what something is worth. You must use the Internet to figure it out yourself.* To put it another way: ask what Aunt Minnie's salad forks are worth in a mailing list and everyone will shun you.

How do figure out their value yourself? There are many Web pages where appraisers and other collectors tell you exactly how to go about this, using the Web as well as published price guides and other sources. (And please don't ask *them* what your aunt's salad forks are worth either.)

You should also keep watch on big auction sites like eBay (**http://www.ebay.com**). Use their search feature to search completed auctions to see what prices items like yours have been selling for. (Don't search current auctions, because people often place bids in the last hour of an auction.) You can also watch the Web sites of dealers who sell similar items.

But keep in mind that many factors determine what price a collectible or antique well sell for. These include:

• The area of the country in which its sold. Prices of collectibles and antiques vary tremendously depending on geography. The Navajo basket that sells for a thousand dollars in a San Francisco gallery may garner only a hundred bucks in the Upper Michigan peninsula.

• The item's condition.

• Whether and how you can prove the item is authentic.

• Current fads and trends that make some collectibles hot and others nearly unsaleable.

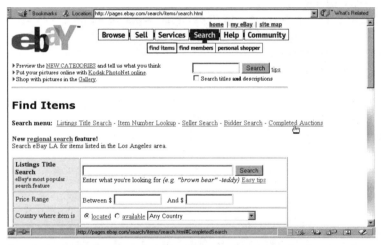

Search the "completed auctions" on Web auction sites to learn prices for which your favorite collectible has recently sold. Prices can vary a lot depending upon everything from the weather on the day that your auction ends (people tend not to log into Web auction sites on sunny weekends) to who happens to be bidding.

Web Sites With Basic Advice on How to Research Collectible Prices If You Haven't a Clue Where to Start

"WHAT IS IT WORTH?"
BY LIZ BRYMAN AT ABOUT.COM
http://costumejewels.about.com/library/blwitw.htm?pid=2740&cob=home

"EVALUATIONS: MANY DIFFERENT WORTHS" BY LIZ BRYMAN
http://costumejewels.about.com/library/weekly/mcurrent.htm?pid=2740&cob=home
also accessible through http://costumejewels.about.com
The ever-opinionated Liz offers solid advice to newbies on how to use the Internet and other resources to research what an "old thing" is worth.

"WHY THEY'RE CALLED PRICE GUIDES"
BY JUDITH KATZ-SCHWARTZ
http://collectorsweb.com/features/priceguides.htm
Well-known appraiser Katz-Schwartz tells you what a published "book price" really means and why it doesn't always tell you how much the piece will sell for.

What Is That Beanie on the Shelf Really Worth?
When we searched three different Web price guides for the price of a particular Beanie Baby randomly plucked from the shelf, we found three different prices. One site claimed it was worth $375, another reported $40, and a third said it was worth only a pitiable $5 to $10. And what was our Beanie selling for on eBay? Ending auction prices ranged from $7 to $25, with most close to $7. (This was after Ty announced that it's discontinuing Beanies.) Moral of the story: Price guides can be helpful, but in the last analysis a collectible is only worth how much you can sell it for.

SARAH LOCKER'S "PLEASE READ THIS FIRST!" FAQ

http://barbiedolls.about.com/library/bl-email.htm?pid=2740&cob=home
http://barbiedolls.about.com

Sarah, who runs the Barbie Doll collecting site at About.Com, tells you how to determine your doll's worth, how to sell it, and why you shouldn't ask her to buy it. Much of her advice is applicable for other types of collectibles.

"HELP! I DON'T KNOW WHAT IT'S WORTH" BY LEE BERNSTEIN

http://members.tripod.com/~vintage_collectibles/archive1-3.html

"FACTORS INFLUENCING VALUE OF COLLECTIBLES" BY LEE BERNSTEIN

http://pages.ebay.com/aw/catindex-collectibles-value.html

"FACTORS INFLUENCING VALUE OF ANTIQUES"

http://pages.ebay.com/community/library/catindex-antiques-value.html

ANTIQUES AS INVESTMENTS, FROM MICROSOFT NETWORK

http://communities.msn.com/antiques/investing.asp

"WHAT IS IT? WHAT IS IT WORTH?"
FROM *COUNTRY LIVING MAGAZINE*

http://www.countryliving.com/
http://homearts.com/cl/collect/89what11.htm

An appraiser identifies collectibles and helps readers determine what they're worth in this popular monthly column.

WHAT'S HOT AND WHAT'S NOT FROM COUNTRY LIVING MAGAZINE

http://homearts.com/cl/toc/00clclc1.htm

Web Sites With Advice for Appraising Specific Types of Collectibles and Antiques

The International Book Collectors Association offers numerous articles on how to determine whether your old books are worth anything.

"APPRAISE YOUR OWN BOOKS"
BY GLENN LARSEN
http://www.rarebooks.org/values.htm
Find out how to determine the worth of your old books in this beginner's guide to book appraisal from The International Book Collectors Association

"THE ESSENTIALS OF COLLECTING"
BY ROBERT F. LUCAS
http://www.rarebooks.org/essentia.htm
Lucas discusses many facets of determining a book's value and collectability in this series of tutorials from the International Book Collectors Association.

"DETERMINING THE VALUE OF OLD POSTCARDS"
http://collectorsweb.com/features/pc.htm

"FACTORS INFLUENCING VALUE OF SPORTS COLLECTIBLES" BY JOHN BUONAGUIDI & GEORGE KENISTON

http://pages.ebay.com/community/library/catindex-sports-value.html

GEM TIPS

http://gemstone.org/tips.html

How to judge gem quality, pricing tips, and the value of certificates are among the topics discussed on this site hosted by the International Colored Gemstone Association.

MARK R. JORDON, INC. AUTOGRAPHS AND MEMORABILIA APPRAISALS AND AUTHENTICATIONS

http://www.markjordan.com/Appraisals.htm

 Free Directories of Price Guides

You'll find price guides for everything from diamonds to cigar box labels at Collector's Universe.

COLLECTOR'S UNIVERSE PRICE GUIDES
http://www.collectors.com
Collector's Universe offers price guides for many, many different collectibles including: advertising, Americana, ancient coins, antiques, art, autographs, banknotes, beanies, books, cigars, modern coins, comic books, cowboy memorabilia, cigars, dolls, diamonds, glass, gold, silver, golf collectibles, guitars, Indian collectibles, magazines, military, minerals, movie memorabilia, paper, photographs, porcelain, pottery, political collectibles, postcards, radio & TV collectibles, science-fiction collectibles, stamps, sports, surfing collectibles, toys, sports memorabilia, watches, trains, toys, and wine.

THE BIG RED TOYBOX PRICE GUIDES
http://www.bigredtoybox.com/price/price.shtml
*The Big Red Toybox (**http://www.bigredtoybox.com**) maintains a huge database of links to price guides around the Web for everything from Hot Wheels to Billy Blastoff and Man from UNCLE collectibles*

BARBIE PRICE GUIDES FROM SARAH LOCKER AT ABOUT.COM
http://barbiedolls.about.com
Sarah Locker at About.Com keeps an extensive list of links to Barbie price guides around the Web at her mega-Barbie Doll site.

BEANIE PRICES
http://www.virtualbeaniebabies.com/prices.html
Look up the price for Goldie the Goldish or Stripes the Tiger at Virtual Beanies.

ALLEYGUIDE HOT WHEELS ONLINE PRICE GUIDE
http://www.alleyguide.com

FROM WORLD WIDE COLLECTORS DIGEST, INC.
http://www.wwcd.com

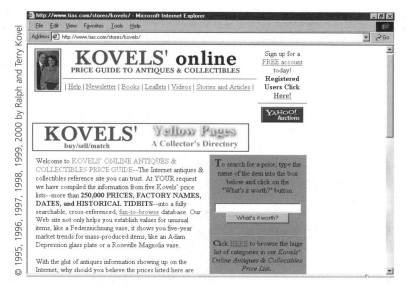

Look up the price for that rare beer can or shaving mug in Kovels' Online Price Guide.

KOVELS' ONLINE PRICE GUIDE FOR ANTIQUES & COLLECTIBLES
http://www.tias.com/stores/kovels
Kovels are among the definitive price guides for collectors. Kovels have compiled prices for nearly a quarter-million collectible items into a database you can search for free. Check out the article "How We List Prices" (**http://www.tias.com/stores/kovels/help.html#8**) *for information on how the guides are compiled.*

PRICE GUIDE — SPORTS MEMORABILIA
http://www.wwcd.com/priceg/mrblpg.html

PRICE GUIDES — TRADING CARDS
http://www.wwcd.com/priceg/tc/priceg-tc-index.html

ARTFACT
http://www.artfact.com
After you register (it's free), you can search a database of art, antiques, collectibles, and jewelry auction sales records. The database offers market value and auction history.

Directories of Appraisers & Advice on Hiring Appraisers

Many of these Web sites offer advice on hiring appraisers, as well as directories of appraisers who specialize in specific types of appraisals. If you're looking for an appraiser you should also ask for recommendations in e-mail discussion lists specific to the type of item you want appraised. (See Chapter 4.)

MAINE ANTIQUE DIGEST APPRAISER DATABASE
http://www.maineantiquedigest.com/appraise/appraise.htm
A searchable database that includes members of the three major American appraisal groups: the American Society of Appraisers, the Appraisers Association of America, and the International Society of Appraisers.

ANTIQUE COLLECTORS CLUB DIRECTORY OF APPRAISERS
http://www.antiquecc.com/addlink/storage/appraiser.html

INTERNATIONAL SOCIETY OF APPRAISERS
http://www.isa-appraisers.org/search.htm

QUILT APPRAISERS
http://www.quilthistory.com/quilt.htm

AMERICAN SOCIETY OF APPRAISERS
http://www.appraisers.org

ANTIQUE COLLECTOR'S CLUB APPRAISER'S LIST
http://www.antiquecc.com/addlink/storage/appraiser.html
A large searchable database of appraisers in many different areas.

HGTV'S "APPRAISAL FAIR" DIRECTORY OF APPRAISERS
http://www.hgtv.com/shows/AFA.shtml
Appraisers who appear on the HGTV show.

MALONEY'S ONLINE
http://www.maloneysonline.com
A free online directory of 18,000 appraisers, clubs, dealers, experts, periodicals, repair services, and suppliers. This is the Web version of the book Maloney's Antiques & Collectibles Resource Directory.

DEBORAH ROBERTS' QUILT APPRAISAL PAGE
http://quilt.com/DebbieRoberts/appraise.htm
Certified quilt appraiser Roberts explains why you should get your quilts appraised and how to hire an appraiser. Her site includes a list of appraisers certified by the American Quilter's Society and who can be e-mailed. These appraisers are qualified to appraise fair market, insurance, and donation values of quilts. Roberts also provides quilt care, labeling, and storage advice.

APPRAISING YOUR QUILTS, PART 1
http://www.shellyquilts.com/appraising-1.htm

APPRAISING YOUR QUILTS, PART II
http://www.shellyquilts.com/appraising-2.htm
Shelly Zegart explains the common types of appraisals, how you find an appraiser, the elements of a correctly prepared appraisal, and more.

QUILTSCAPE: APPRAISALS
http://www.quiltscape.com/Appraisers/appraisers.html
A directory of appraisers certified by the American Quilters Society.

Free Advice on Insuring Your Collection

"INSURING YOUR COLLECTION" FROM EBAY
http://pages.ebay.com/aw/catindex-collectibles-insuring.html

INSURING YOUR JEWELRY
http://jewelleryappraisals.com/hwinsure.htm
Learn how much—and what type of coverage you need.

free Advice on Cleaning, Storing & Repairing Your Antiques & Collectibles

Whether you collect crystal figurines or pocket watches, your biggest chore as a collector is properly storing, cleaning, and repairing your treasures. You can't trust the advice of just anyone when it comes to keeping your Beanies dust-free or cleaning the green gunk off Barbie's ears. The best source of advice on cleaning and repairing collectibles is other collectors. We recommend joining some of the mailing lists recommended in Chapter 4 or tapping into the Usenet discussion groups to find cleaning and repair advice specific to the items you collect. In fact, you'll often find controversies raging in these groups on how best to clean rhinestones or preserve quilts made of feathers. In this chapter, you'll find Web sites that offer general advice on cleaning and restoring collectibles and antiques. In the following chapter you'll find Web sites that offer advice on caring for specific items.

Free General Restoration and Conservation Web Guides

CARING FOR YOUR TREASURES
http://palimpsest.stanford.edu/aic/treasure
Stanford University runs this big Web site, where you'll find lots of advice on caring for architecture, paintings, furniture, home videotapes, textiles, and books. There's also a section on framing works of art, plus information on the American Institute for Conservation of Historic and Artistic Works.

THE ANTIQUE DOCTOR AT ANTIQUE RESOURCES
http://www.antiqueresources.com/doc.html
Readers write in describing their ailing antiques and the doctor provides advice on how to fix them.

"CARING FOR YOUR COLLECTION" BY LEE BERNSTEIN
http://pages.ebay.com/aw/catindex-collectibles-caring.html

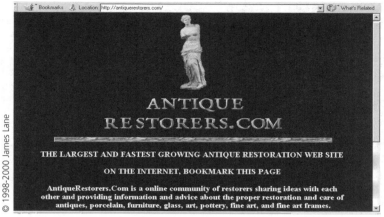

Find answers to your furniture and upholstery restoration questions plus cleaning and stain removal advice at AntiqueRestorers.Com.

ANTIQUERESTORERS.COM
http://antiquerestorers.com

Whether you're refinishing an oak sidebar or fixing a candlestick, this huge Web site should be your first stop. It offers hundreds of articles on restoration of furniture, upholstery, ceramics, and textiles, plus message boards, links to restoration advice around the Internet, and a whole lot more. It also offers a database of professional restorers.

AMERICAN CONSERVATION CONSORTIUM, LTD
http://pw1.netcom.com/~artcons

This is the Web site of a professional conservation service, but it offers worthwhile articles on topics like wood furniture care.

Find a Restorer Through Recommendations from Other Collectors on the Web *Looking for someone to fix that broken toy train or restore Grandma's dress mannequin to presentability? Your best bet is to ask for recommendations of professional restorers through mailing lists or other discussion groups devoted to your collectible. Not all restorers are equally skilled. A poor one can reduce your treasured collectible to unsightly junk. Be sure to get lots of recommendations and check references of satisfied customers.*

CONSERVATION ONLINE (COOL)
FROM STANFORD UNIVERSITY
http://palimpsest.stanford.edu

The Stanford Preservation Department offers one of the largest Internet resources for preservation advice. You'll find links to organizations and sellers of preservation products, plus a database covering a wide range of conservation topics.

ANTIQUE RESOURCES' RESTORATION FEATURES
http://www.antiqueresources.com/restoration/index.html

How do you clean porcelain? How do you find a reputable restorer? Do instant glues drive you crazy? Antique Resources offers a library of articles on repair topics.

RESTORATION SERVICES AND SUPPLIES
http://collectors.org/doc/repairs.asp

You'll find a wide variety of repair and cleaning tips for items including alabaster, books, bottles, gold, jewelry, leather, linens, needlework, textiles, metals, photographs, tinware, and woodenware. You'll also find information on groups and associations serving the restoration industry, plus advice on how to find a reputable restorer.

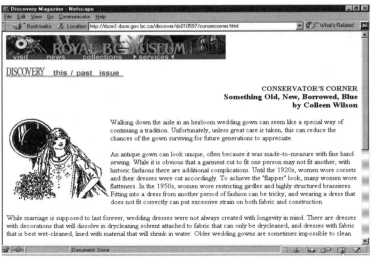

Read conservation tips from the Royal British Columbia Museum at their Web site at **http://rbcm1.rbcm.gov.bc.ca**.

NORTHERN STATES CONSERVATION CENTER
http://www.collectioncare.org

Tap into articles on over 200 preservation topics from storage to pest control.

"TEN TIPS FOR CARE OF WATER-DAMAGED FAMILY HEIRLOOMS" FROM BUTTERFIELD & BUTTERFIELD AUCTION HOUSE
http://www.butterfields.com/online/magazineB1aleft.html

RESTORATION ARTICLES FROM THE ASSOCIATION OF RESTORERS
http://www.assoc-restorers.com/r-articles

Get Preservation Help from the U.S. Government
Want to find out how to remove grafitti from historic masonry? Need advice on repairing historic ornamental plaster or stained glass? The **National Park Service** offers dozens of incredible articles on restoring historic homes (**http://www2.cr.nps.gov/tps/briefs/presbhom.htm**) on its Web site. Another terrific government site to check out is **Saving America's Treasures** (**http://www.saveam-ericastreasures.org**). A joint project of the White House Millennium Council and the National Trust for Historic Preservation, the organization's goal is the preservation of cultural treasures including documents, works of art, maps, journals, and buildings.

ANTIQUE COLLECTING ARTICLES
http://www.antiquecc.com/articles/index.html
A collection of articles from Antique Collecting Magazine, *including ones on clock restoration, ceramic conservation, textile conservation, and many other topics.*

THE CONSERVATOR'S CORNER,
BY COLLEEN WILSON
Colleen Wilson, a conservator at the Royal British Columbia Museum, offers preservation tips on a variety of subjects in her column in the museum's Discovery *magazine. You can read it on their Web site (http://rbcm1.rbcm.gov.bc.ca/discover/issues.html). Here's a guide to past columns:*

"The Care and Feeding of Baskets"
by Colleen Wilson
http://rbcm1.rbcm.gov.bc.ca/discover/ds26996/cnfeedb.html

"Recipe for Leather Care"
http://rbcm1.rbcm.gov.bc.ca/discover/ds24596/conserve.html

"Hi-Ho, Silver Tarnish Away"
http://rbcm1.rbcm.gov.bc.ca/discover/ds24295/6-silver.html

"Plastics Forever?"
http://rbcm1.rbcm.gov.bc.ca/discover/ds190397/cc-plastics.html

"Something Old, Something New"
http://rbcm1.rbcm.gov.bc.ca/discover/ds010597/consercorner.html

"A Stitch In Time: Framing Old Needlework"
http://rbcm1.rbcm.gov.bc.ca/discover/ds150197/stitchintime.html

"How Light It Grows"
http://rbcm1.rbcm.gov.bc.ca/discover/ds241196/howlight.html

"Fur Futures"
http://rbcm1.rbcm.gov.bc.ca/discover/ds030399/ccorner.html

"Storing Old Photographs"
http://rbcm1.rbcm.gov.bc.ca/discover/ds310898/ccorner.html

"Storing War Medals"
http://rbcm1.rbcm.gov.bc.ca/discover/ds011198/conservcorner.html

"Treasured Textiles"
http://rbcm1.rbcm.gov.bc.ca/notes/textiles.html

CONSERVATION HELP FROM THE BISHOP MUSEUM IN HAWAII

"Understanding Lacquer"
http://www.bishop.hawaii.org/bishop/conservation/lacquer.html

"Bugs Are Eating My Family Treasures"
http://www.bishop.hawaii.org/bishop/conservation/bugs_eating.html

"Having Your Works of Art Paper Matted and Framed"
http://www.bishop.hawaii.org/bishop/conservation/mats.html

"The Care of Silver"
http://www.bishop.hawaii.org/bishop/conservation/silver.html

"Wet-Cleaning Quilts at Home"
http://www.bishop.hawaii.org/bishop/conservation/quilts.html

"The Care of Feathers"
http://www.bishop.hawaii.org/bishop/conservation/feathers.html

"Archival Mounts for Paintings on Textiles"
http://www.bishop.hawaii.org/bishop/conservation/painttextiles.html

ASSOCIATION OF RESTORERS FORUMS AND CHAT
http://www.assoc-restorers.com/forums
A large selection of articles by members of the Association of Restorers. There are articles on using wood bleach, repairing furniture joints, how to clean fine porcelain, silver and ceramic restoration, and more. Post your restoration questions in the chat forums.

 Free Advice on Displaying Your Collection

"DISPLAYING YOUR COLLECTION" BY LEE BERNSTEIN
http://pages.ebay.com/aw/catindex-collectibles-display.html

"DISPLAYING ANTIQUES" FROM EBAY
http://pages.ebay.com/community/library/
catindex-antiques-display.html

CHAPTER 8

free Advice on Caring for & Cleaning Specific Kinds of Antiques & Collectibles

There is an art to repairing any cherished object. Whether it's a plaster bookend or a ceramic mug, if you botch the repair, you mar the item's beauty as well as its value. The Web is full of secrets on how to care for, clean, and repair fragile objects. Did you know that if you boil in cream of tartar old linen that's as brown as gravy it may whiten to an antique cream? Did you know that the best way to remove "green gunk" from old costume jewelry is to dab it with ketchup? This chapter covers Web sites that offer repair and restoration advice for furniture, glass, textiles, toys, clocks, books, radios, papers, jewelry, and even antique hand fans. In fact, we think that you may find this to be the most valuable chapter in the book. The sites that we've listed are only the tip of restoration advice available on the Internet. We also strongly suggest that you tap into a mailing list discussion group about your collecting passion for expert restoration help from other collectors and professionals. To find them head to Chapter 4.

Free Help Repairing and Restoring Furniture and Other Wooden Things

"IS YOUR FURNITURE IN BLOOM?"
http://collectorsweb.com/features/bloom.htm
How to remove white spots when moisture has penetrated a lacquer or shellac finish.

"REPAIRING A CRACKED HEADBOARD"
FROM *FINE WOODWORKING MAGAZINE*
http://www.taunton.com/fw/features/techniques/39headboard.htm

"REPLACING A SPINDLE IN A CHAIR BACK"
FROM *FINE WOODWORKING MAGAZINE*
http://www.taunton.com/fw/features/techniques/12rplcspndl.htm

"SHOULD ANTIQUE FURNITURE BE FED LINSEED OIL?" FROM *FINE WOODWORKING MAGAZINE*

http://www.taunton.com/fw/features/techniques/27linseed.htm
Tips on preserving antique finishes without using linseed oil.

FURNITURE REFINISHING Q&A FROM ANTIQUE RESOURCES

http://www.antiqueresources.com/articles/refinishqa.html
Fred Lichtenwalter offers advice on refinishing tables, pianos, wagons, and other pieces of ailing furniture in this regular feature from AntiqueResources.Com.

A BEGINNER'S GUIDE TO ANTIQUE FURNITURE REFINISHING BY FRED LICHTENWALTER

http://www.antiqueresources.com/articles/refinish-1.html
http://www.antiqueresources.com/articles/refinish-2.html
http://www.antiqueresources.com/articles/refinish-3.html
http://www.antiqueresources.com/articles/refinish-4.html
http://www.antiqueresources.com/articles/refinish-5.html
http://www.antiqueresources.com/articles/refinish-6.html
http://www.antiqueresources.com/articles/refinish-7.html
Before you whip out that can of furniture refinisher, read this eye-opening seven-part series that covers everything from stripper to stains. Be sure to read all of Fred's safety advice before starting.

"SAVING THE FINISH ON YOUR WOODEN ITEMS" BY JEFF JEWITT

http://www.antiqueresources.com/articles/finish_saving.html
Jeff offers advice on whether to save or strip the finish in this article from AntiqueResources.Com.

MUSICAL INSTRUMENT CONSERVATION MAILING LIST

http://palimpsest.stanford.edu/byform/mailing-lists/micat
If antique violas and tubas are your thing, sign up for this mailing list discussion group—and read archives of past messages on restoration at this Web site.

FURNITURE AND WOODEN OBJECT PRESERVATION AND CARE

http://pweb.netcom.com/~artcons/care.html
Marc A. Williams at American Conservation Consortium explains how proper maintenance will slow deterioration.

ANTIQUE FURNITURE RESTORATION
http://www.steeltower.com/c/restoration
Luis Stortini Sabor explains the materials and techniques used in furniture restoration.

THE FURNITURE WIZARD
http://www.furniturewizard.com
Plenty of information on the restoration of antiques, furniture repair, and refinishing.

 Free Help Cleaning and Storing Glass, Pottery & Ceramics

"CLEANING POTTERY" BY JERRY MCCRACKEN
http://www.antiqueresources.com/articles/pottclean.html
A detailed how-to, full of do's, don'ts, and other bits of wisdom.

"CERAMIC RESTORATION AND CONSERVATION" BY LAWRENCE BRADSHAW
http://www.antiqueresources.com/articles/ceramicrestore.html
Lawrence discusses the different methods of ceramic repair in depth.

"ARE WATER STAINS CLOUDING YOUR VIEW?"
http://collectorsweb.com/features/waterstain.htm
Tips on removing water stains from glass.

SENSING CERAMIC DEFECTS
http://www.pbs.org/wgbh/pages/roadshow/tips/china_defects.html
David Lackey of Houston's David Lackey Antiques explains how to use your eyes, ears, and sense of touch to ascertain ceramic defects.

"A PROFESSIONAL METHOD FOR CLEANING OPTICS" BY ROBERT ARIAIL, FROM *THE JOURNAL OF THE ANTIQUE TELESCOPE SOCIETY*
http://www1.tecs.com/oldscope/atspages/techtips.htm

 *Free Help Cleaning and Repairing Textiles*

"CONSERVATION OF TEXTILE ITEMS" BY SHIRLEY NIEMEYER AND PATRICIA COX CREWS
http://www.ianr.unl.edu/pubs/NebFacts/NF137.HTM
This University of Nebraska Extension article offers advice on cleaning, care, storage, and display of treasured textiles.

THE RESOURCE: TEXTILES, CLOTHING & DESIGN
http://www.ianr.unl.edu/pubs/Textiles
The University of Nebraska Cooperative Extension offers advice on handling the sorts of stains and odors that often infect rural quilts: skunk perfume, pesticide stench, smoke odors, and mildew.

INTERNATIONAL FAN COLLECTOR'S GUILD CONSERVATION RESOURCES
http://www.hand-fan.org/FANwebsite/resources/
conservation_choices.htm
http://www.hand-fan.org
You'll find a wide variety of information on preserving and caring for antique fans, including their laces and ivory.

ASK MRS. BIDDINGTON — LACE RESTORATION
http://www.biddingtons.com/content/mrslace.html
Mrs. Biddington explains that learning how to restore lace first requires one to know how the lace is constructed. Then she goes into details.

THE QUILTBROKER
http://www.quiltbroker.com/quilt_storage.html
Should you wrap your quilts in buffered or unbuffered acid-free tissue? Should you store your quilts on tubes? The QuiltBroker answers such questions and many more on its quilt storage information page.

ILLINOIS COUNTRY STITCHERS' TEXTILE PRESERVATION RESOURCES
http://www.prairienet.org/community/clubs/quilts/pres.html
and
http://www.prairienet.org/quilts/preserve.html
This Champaign, Illinois quilting guild offers a list of Web sites devoted to textile preservation and a bibliography of good books on preservation, many published by museums.

THE KIRK COLLECTION—RESTORATION SERVICES
http://kirkcollection.com
http://kirkcollection.com/restoration_services.asp

CLEANING ANTIQUE QUILTS
http://www.quilthistory.com/cleaning.htm
Learn how to test fabrics for bleeding and how to make a butter-milk recipe to clean your antique quilts.

WORLD WIDE QUILTING'S QUILT CARE ADVICE
http://ttsw.com/HowTo/QuiltCare.html

WORLD WIDE QUILTING'S STAIN REMOVAL FAQ
http://quilt.com/FAQS/StainRemovalFAQ.html
Sue Traudt's World Wide Quilting Web site offers a collection of ideas and comments on quilt care, gathered from members of the QuiltNet mailing list discussion group, AOL Quilters Online, and Usenet. Subjects include washing quilts and handling faded fabrics.

QUILT STORAGE AND DISPLAY ADVICE FROM DAWN DUPERAULT
http://www.redsword.com/dduperault/storage.htm

TEXTILES CONSERVATION MAILING LIST
http://palimpsest.stanford.edu/byform/mailing-lists/texcons
Sign up for this discussion group devoted to preservation of antique textiles. You can also read the archives of past messages.

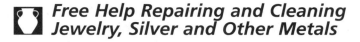

Free Help Repairing and Cleaning Jewelry, Silver and Other Metals

SPARKLES' CLEANING & REPAIR TIPS FOR VINTAGE COSTUME JEWELRY

http://www.sparkleplenty.com/info/clean.htm

Learn to clean and reset rhinestones (don't dunk them in water), how to remove "green gunk," how to fix broken pin-backs and more.

ISABELLE BRYMAN'S JEWELRY CLEANING & REPAIR LINKS & ADVICE AT ABOUT.COM

http://costumejewels.about.com

http://costumejewels.about.com/library/weekly/aa040698.htm?pid=2740&cob=home

Liz offers the consummate Internet resource on repairing and cleaning vintage costume jewelry.

CLEANING & REPAIRING JEWELRY

http://pages.ebay.com/aw/catindex-jewelry-caring.html

"RECIPES FOR CLEANING GOLD & SILVER JEWELRY BY TAMMY POWLEY, JEWELRY-MAKING GUIDE AT ABOUT.COM

http://jewelrymaking.about.com/library/blclean.htm?pid=2740&cob=home

http://jewelrymaking.about.com

"PROPER CARE OF GEMSTONES" BY THE TRADE SHOP

http://www.tradeshop.com/gems/care.html

COYOTE CREEK'S ADVICE ON CLEANING & STORING INDIAN AND SILVER JEWELRY

http://www.coyotecreek.com/CCSP13.html

REED & BARTON'S CARING FOR SILVER GUIDE

http://www.reedandbarton.com

The care tips offered by this silver maker include "Don't wash silver in lemon-scented dish soap" and "Wash silver separately from stainless steel flatware."

"CARING FOR SILVER" BY JEFFREY HERMAN
http://www.antiqueresources.com/articles/care.htm
Herman offers a wealth of advice on products to use (and not use) to clean silver, and also offers advice on storing it and keeping it tarnish-free.

SOCIETY OF AMERICAN SILVERSMITH'S SILVER CARE GUIDE
http://www.silversmithing.com/care.htm

"TIPS FOR CLEANING TIN" COMPILED BY MIKE REILLY
http://www.usadvertising.com/tin_cleaning.html

For Jewelry Repair and Preservation Supplies, Tap Into B'Sue's Boutiques
B'Sue's not only offers advice and directions for repairing vintage jewelry and other accessories but also sells just about everything you need to keep your rhinestone broaches glittering and your beaded purses swinging (**http://www.webjewels.com/adornment/supplies.htm**).

 Free Help Repairing and Restoring Dolls and Other Toys

DOLL REPAIR FAQ BY GARY SOWATZKA
http://www.sowatzka.com/gary/repairqa.htm
Read answers to questions such as this one: "I have a 1920's chalk 'piano baby' doll that is painted. She is dirty. What is the best way to clean her without disturbing the paint?" Be sure to click the previous questions and answers link.

HOMESTEAD DOLL HOSPITAL
http://www.webdolls.com/Homestead_collectibles/faq.htm
Learn how to clean vinyl dolls, wash doll hair, wash clothes, and clean mold off dolls.

"'GREEN EAR': THE CAUSE, THE CURE,"
FROM SARAH LOCKER AT ABOUT.COM
http://barbiedolls.about.com/library/weekly/aa050299.htm?pid=274
0&cob=home

Barbie-doll "green ear" is a malady that afflicts many dolls. It's staining of the vintage plastic caused by metal earrings. This page discusses all the products which will remove it, offers advice and cautions, and provides advice for specific vintages of dolls.

TOOLS AND TIPS FOR DOLLY AND ME
http://www.huncamunca.org/toolsandtips.htm
Learn how to create "tressy" looks and Hollywood hairdos on yourself and your dolls.

ASK MRS. BIDDINGTON—DOLL HAIR CARE
http://www.biddingtons.com/content/mrsdollhair.html
Learn about the care and cleaning of doll hair.

G.I. JOE MEDIC
http://gijoemedic.com/default.htm
Learn about the "medic" services performed by Joe DeGrella and his wife, Susie; view pictures of repairs; and read tips in the "Physical Therapy" area such as "never twist the body." There's also an extensive list of G.I. Joe-related links.

Looking for a doll hospital? Or thinking about rerooting Barbie's hair your-self? Visit Melissa Beck's forum on Suite101.Com for doll-fixing advice and to chat with other doll fixers.

DOLL REPAIR AT SUITE101.COM
http://www.suite101.com/welcome.cfm/doll_repair
Melissa Beck runs this marvelous Web site where you'll learn all the fine points of doll repair—from how to repair your vintage doll without ruining its value to how to replace Barbie's lost swimsuit.

KRISTA'S DOLL RESTORATION FAQS
http://www.dollrestoration.com/QandA.htm
Krista covers all the basics for caring for Barbie and other vintage vinyl and "mod" dolls, including cleaning vinyl, caring for acces-sories, storing and displaying dolls, and restyling hair. The site includes before-and-after photos.

G.I. JOE RESTORATION & REPAIR
http://members.aol.com/gitrooper/howto/index.htm
From saving scuba suits to pressing uniforms, it's all here in this information-laden FAQ from G.I. Trooper. The advice is applicable to other dolls.

SHER'S DOLL DOCTOR
http://www.srhein.simplenet.com/dolldoctor.html
http://www.srhein.simplenet.com/Repair.html
Sher offers tips on repairing vinyl dolls; fixing "Barbie bad hair days" by restyling, dyeing, and rerooting hair; and more.

Read About the History of Dolls and Other "Things" in Our Lives by Heading to These Informative Web Sites
At **Decades of Dolls from Kaylee's Korner of Collectible Dolls (http://www.dollinfo.com/ballons.htm)** you can view photographs and descriptions of dolls from the Thirties through the Nineties. At **About.com (http://collectdolls.about.com)**, you can read the informative "A Brief History of Antique Dolls" by Denise van Patten. There's an assortment of articles on topics relating to the 19th century, including Civil War era wedding gowns and corsets from the 1881 Lord & Taylor catalogue, at the **Victoriana Study Center (http://www.victorian.com/library/direct.html)**. You can read about the lives, homes, clothing, food, and tools of Colonial America at **The Colonial Williamsburg Foundation (http://www.history.org)**.

REPAIRING AND RESTORING DOLLIKINS
http://home.att.net/~dollikin/hints.html

Learn how to reroot hair, tighten wrist joints, and fix cracks or chips.

THE BEAUTY PARLOR
FROM KAYLEE'S CORNER OF COLLECIBLE DOLLS
http://www.dollinfo.com/caretips.htm

A collection of doll cleaning and restoration tips covering composition, hard plastic, vinyl, wigs, and clothing.

⚙ Free Help Repairing and Restoring Clocks, Radios and Other Mechanical Things

CONDITION CLASSIFICATION GUIDE FOR ANTIQUE TOOLS
http://www.mwtca.org/images/classf.gif
Learn how to preserve and repair your old tools in this FAQ from the Tool Collector's Club.

VINTAGE RADIO REPAIR & RESTORATION
http://www.vintage-radio.com
You'll find loads of technical information from "How Do Those Funny Glass Things Work?" to tips on tackling AM and FM alignment. You'll also find technical history and advice on how to restore cabinets. Tutorials show you how to build your own test equipment.

NOSTALGIA AIR
http://www.nostalgiaair.org
http://www.nostalgiaair.org/NostalgiaAir/Articles/index.htm
Nostalgia Air offers lots of information on restoring old radios and their cabinets. The tutorials span every subject imaginable, from testing transformers to replacing line cords.

ANTIQUE RADIOS ONLINE RESTORATION DISCUSSION BOARD
http://antiqueradios.com/forum
Learn how to restore antique radios and cabinets (and other antique furniture as well) in the message boards of Antique Radios Online.

ANTIQUE RADIO GRILLE CLOTH
http://www.grillecloth.com
Everything you need to know about radio grille cloth, including where to buy it and how to install it. The site includes a directory of links to information on antique radio restoration.

THE ATMOS CLOCK MANUAL
BY MICHAEL P. MURRAY:
http://www.webcom.com/~z4murray/atmocare.html
A complete manual covering locking the pendulum, leveling the clock, trouble-shooting, storing and shipping, estimating value, and more.

CLOCK RESTORATION BY JULIE TARGETT
http://www.artbookservices.com/articles/april97/Apr97_5.html

CARE OF OLD CLOCKS
http://antiqueclocks.com/care.htm
Basic antique clock adjusting, care, and maintenance tips from The Internet Clock Shop.

RESTORATION OF NIKON CAMERAS
http://www.nikonhs.org/tech_articles/restore.html
Fred Krughoff explains how to tell if restoration is appropriate and offers valuable guidance such as "never repaint or rechrome and never lubricate."

THE CARE OF MACHINES
http://www.ismacs.net/articles/restoration.html
The International Sewing Machine Collectors Society explains how to care for your sewing machine.

THE MIDWEST TOOL COLLECTOR'S
ENCYCLOPEDIA OF TOOL COLLECTING
http://www.mwtca.org/otc

Learn How the Arts & Crafts Movement Changed Interior Design
At Tom Stermitz's **Mission Style Antiques, Craftsman Style Architecture, & the Ragtime Era** Web site (**http://www.csn.net/ragtime/Ragtime_Index.html**) you can learn all about the influence of this decorative design movement that was concerned with objects of use.

Free Help Storing and Preserving Paper Items

INTERNATIONAL BOOK COLLECTORS ASSOCIATION
http://www.rarebooks.org

*You'll find information on preserving books, leather, and paper and the proper care and handling of old books. The IBCA's FAQ on book preservation (**http://www.rarebooks.org/questions.htm**), offers advice on what to do with wet books, how to get rid of mildew stains and smells, how to dispel bugs, and whether to oil leather.*

THE LIBRARY OF CONGRESS PRESERVATION
http://lcweb.loc.gov/preserv

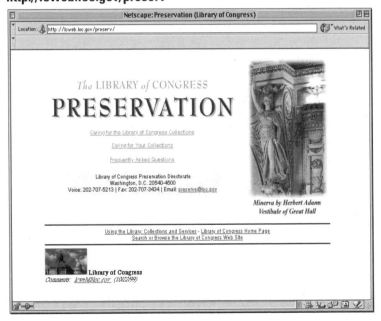

CONSERVATION FRAMER'S MAILING LIST
http://palimpsest.stanford.edu/byform/mailing-lists/framecon
http://www.egroups.com/group/frameconnews

Find out how to sign up for this discussion group for framers, plus read archives of past messages.

BOOK_ARTS-L MAILING LIST
http://palimpsest.stanford.edu/byform/mailing-lists/bookarts
The Book_Arts-L discussion group is for anyone interested in preserving and caring for books. This list is run from Syracuse University. You can sign up by sending an e-mail to: listserv@listserv.syr.edu. *The message should read:* subscribe book_arts-l yourfirstname yourlastname
*You can read past messages from the list at the BookArts Web site (*http://www.dreamscape.com/pdverhey*).*

NEWSPAPER PRESERVATION RECIPE
http://collectorsweb.com/features/newspaper.htm

CARE OF OLD PHOTOGRAPHS
http://www.kawartha.net/~jleonard/care.htm
Learn about the factors that speed up damage to photographs, storing photographs, and ways (such as repairing tears with tape) in which photos are mistreated.

DARTMOUTH COLLEGE LIBRARY: A SIMPLE BOOK REPAIR MANUAL
http://www.dartmouth.edu/~preserve/tofc.html
A complete manual on book repair, including book cleaning, dealing with torn pages, hinge repair, and more.

SALVAGE OPERATIONS FOR WATER DAMAGED COLLECTIONS, BY BETTY WALSH
http://palimpsest.stanford.edu/waac/wn/wn10/wn10-2/wn10-202.html

Do you have bugs, mold, or wet records? Don't panic. Visit The National Archives and Records Administration Questions about Disaster Prevention and Recovery (**http://www.nara.gov/arch/faqs/aboutdis.html**) for advice and resources.

NORTHEAST DOCUMENT CONSERVATION CENTER—FREQUENTLY ASKED QUESTIONS ABOUT PRESERVATION
http://www.nedcc.org/faqpres.htm
Learn how to remove the musty smell from old books, how to store photographs and papers, how long laser-printed documents will last, how to treat wooden bookcases to make them safe for storing historical documents, and how to care for old leather books.

NORTHEAST DOCUMENT CONSERVATION—CARE OF PHOTOGRAPHS
http://www.nedcc.org/phocar.htm
Learn about the common factors affecting the permanence of all photographs.

NORTHEAST DOCUMENT CONSERVATION—PRESERVING FAMILY COLLECTIONS
http://www.nedcc.org/fmlycol.htm
A list of recommendations and resources for preserving family documents and memorabilia.

CARING FOR YOUR COLLECTION
http://lcweb.loc.gov/preserv/careothr.html

Find Historic Photos in the Library of Congress's Web Archive
Head to the **American Memory—Historical Collections for the National Digital Library** (**http://memory.loc.org**) to see photos, including ones from the Civil War, baseball, and daguerrotype collections. This is a huge collection with many wonderful things.

free Advice on Buying, Selling and Tracking Down Hard-to-Find Collectibles and Antiques

Who can forget those Saturdays spent shopping with Mom? Remember all the care she took to point out that one should examine the inside of drawers when shopping for a dresser, hold mirrors to the light to make sure they glistened evenly, or look for the "sterling" stamp on silver? And will you ever forget the time she dickered a salesman down $500 on the price of a piano? Don't you wish Mom could accompany you on all your shopping forays through cyberspace? Here are a gaggle of Web sites that offer advice on searching for, buying, and selling collectibles both on the Web and off. We've also included Web sites that offer advice on authenticating collectibles.

✋ ***Warning!*** *Web auction sites are ridden with forgeries of collectibles—especially autographs. Your best defense is to learn as much as possible about how to identify the objects that you collect. In the case of autographs, many warn that you can be sure an autograph is legitimate only if you see the celebrity sign it.*

 ## *Free Advice on Tracking Down Hard-to-Find Collectibles and Antiques*

"I CAN'T FIND MY DOLLY!"
BY SARAH LOCKER AT ABOUT.COM
http://barbiedolls.about.com/library/weekly/mcurrent.htm?pid=274 0&cob=home
How to track down the Barbie doll you want.

TERRIFIC TOY TRACKING TACTICS
http://www.toymania.com/beginnersguide/tips.shtml
How to find that hard-to-find toy that you (or your child) absolutely must have.

Free Advice on Selling Collectibles on the Web

"SELLING AUTOGRAPHS–THE RIGHT WAY"
BY JOHN REZNIKOFF & DEBORAH L. MARCUS
http://www.odysseygroup.com/acm599/dealer.htm

"TO NET OR NOT TO NET, ONE DEALER'S OPINION"
BY RITA PERLOFF
http://www.tias.com/news/5-13-98A.shtml

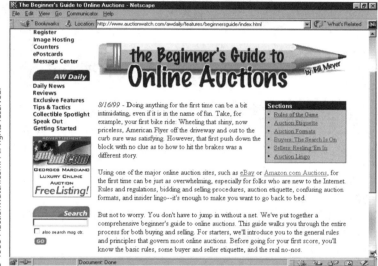

Auction Watch offers an introduction to selling on Web auction sites for those new to the game.

THE BEGINNER'S GUIDE TO AUCTIONS
http://www.auctionwatch.com/awdaily/features/beginnersguide/index.html
Auction Watch offers tips and a primer on getting started selling on Web auction sites.

"TIPS FOR LISTING AND SELLING COLLECTIBLES ON EBAY" BY LEE BERNSTEIN

http://pages.ebay.com/aw/catindex-collectibles-selling.html

Learn how to get the best possible price for your historical autographs and certificates.

FROM THE WASHINGTON HISTORICAL AUTOGRAPH AND CERTIFICATION ORGANIZATION: HOW TO SELL HISTORICAL AUTOGRAPHS AND CERTIFICATIONS

http://www.whaco.com/how2sell.htm

What Do You Do With Old Stock or Bond Certificates? Here are two sites that will help you determine the worth of your holdings. **Researching Old Securities** (**http://www.scripophily.com/research.htm**) from Bob Kerstein, president of Scripophily, provides many excellent resources, information on how to prove ownership, and a listing with links to state securities regulators. **Goldsheet Mining Directory of Obsolete Securities** (**http://goldsheet.simplenet.com/obsolete.htm**) details state, federal, search firms, dealers, and organizations.

Free Advice on Buying Collectibles on the Web & Elsewhere

BARBARA CREW'S ABOUT.COM BUYING/SELLING FEATURES
http://collectibles.about.com/library/articles/aa102897.htm?pid=2740&cob=home
also accessible at http://collectibles.about.com
Barbara offers regular features and tips on buying and selling on Web auctions at her collectibles site on About.Com.

THE EBAY NEW USER'S TUTORIAL
http://pages.ebay.com/aw/wagon.html

RALPH & TERRY KOVELS' ADVICE
http://www.tias.com/stores/kovels/info/news/HomeArticle.html
The Kovels offer news and tips on Internet collectibles scams, misrepresentations, and rip-offs.

"BUYING JEWELS ON THE NET: WHAT TO EXPECT OR NOT" BY ISABELLE BRYMAN
http://costumejewels.about.com/library/weekly/aa120198.htm
Isabelle offers tips on buying vintage costume jewelry, plus a guide to Web shops where you can search for your heart's desire.

BUYING ANTIQUE JEWELRY: DON'T BE BEDAZZLED
http://www.pbs.org/wgbh/pages/roadshow/tips/jewelry.html

FROM WHACO: HOW TO BUY HISTORICAL AUTOGRAPHS AND CERTIFICATIONS, PART I
http://www.whaco.com/how2-1.htm

HOW TO BUY, PART II
http://www.whaco.com/how2-2.htm

FROM WHACO: PREPARING FOR AN AUCTION
http://www.whaco.com/auctprep.htm

◆ Free Advice on Authenticating Collectibles

EBAY'S ADVICE ON AUTHENTICATION OF COLLECTIBLES
http://pages.ebay.com/services/safeharbor/
safeharbor-auth-overview.html

http://pages.ebay.com/services/safeharbor

ANTIQUE & COLLECTORS REPRODUCTION NEWS
http://www.repronews.com

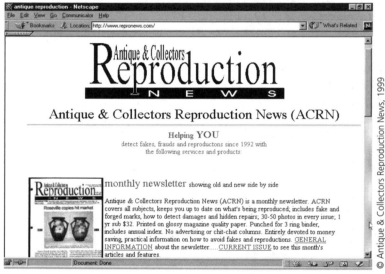

Find out the latest about repros and fakes at the Web site of Antique & Collectors Reproduction News.

This is a for-pay newsletter, but the Web site offers some advice and good reading.

M.I. HUMMEL MARKS OF AUTHENTICITY
http://www.mihummel.com/reference/reference_marks.html

JAPANESE SWORD AUTHENTICATION— IS IT REAL? IS IT OLD?
http://www.gemlink.com/~rstein/realold.htm

INTERNATIONAL NIPPON COLLECTORS' CLUB—REPRODUCTION ALERT

http://www.nipponcollectorsclub.com/reprod.html

Learn about reproductions being passed off as originals.

NIPPON COLLECTORS BEWARE

http://www.noritake.co.jp/nippon/collectors_e.html

View authentic seals and imitations and read guidelines to recognizing imitations.

PRUSSIAN THOUGHTS—FAKES

http://www.rsprussia.com/articles/fakes/reprojunk.html

R.H.Capers explains how to distinguish reproduction junk from authentic Prussian marks.

Look for the Better Business Bureau and eTrust Logos on Web Shopping Sites Have reservations about shopping on the Web? Look for Web stores that feature the Better Business Bureau's logo. If you click on the logo you'll arrive at a BBB Web site with details about the store's reliability. The criteria a store must meet to earn this logo are high. If you spot an eTrust's "TRUSTe" logo, it means that the store has worked with the non-profit group eTrust to develop a public privacy statement about how they will use personal information that you provide to the site in the course of shopping, like address and phone number. Every Web site's privacy statement is different, so be sure to read the one on the Web site before you buy. What about other "safe shopping logos"? They're not as valuable as the BBB's. In fact some aren't more than "fishing licenses"; a store pays $25 and can post the logo on their Web site. The service may not even do any monitoring or follow-up on consumer complaints.

IDENTIFYING THE #1 BARBIE® DOLL
http://www.littledoll.com/id/id.html

© Karen Morley 1999/2000

Do you have one of the original Barbies? The Little Doll tells you how to identify these dolls and even shows pictures of the unique feet and eyes.

Learn the identifying marks of the first Barbie doll, which was introduced at Toy Fair in New York City in 1959.

If you plan to buy or sell collectibles and antiques on the Web, there's really nothing like a mailing list discussion group for soliciting advice on the rudiments of doing business in cyberspace. See Chapter 4 for tips on how to find a mailing list devoted to your collecting passion.

Learn how to use a black light to spot a fake, repairs, and reproductions. Visit **Black Light Flashlight** (**http://www.quickness.com/~blacklight**).

Web Sites that Offer Authentication and Certification Services

REAL BEANS (BEANIES)
http://www.realbeans.com

PROFESSIONAL COIN GRADING SERVICE
http://www.pcgs.com

PROFESSIONAL SPORTS AUTHENTICATOR (TRADING CARDS & AUTOGRAPHS)
http://www.psacard.com

EVERYTHING COLLECTIBLE AUTHENTICATION SERVICE
http://www.everythingcollectible.com/home.html

See Chapter 6 for Web sites with information on finding and hiring appraisers.

In the **National Stolen Art File** (**http://www.fbi.gov/majcases/arttheft/art.htm**), you'll find pictures and descriptions of stolen art posted by the FBI.

Post Pictures on Auction Sites with Free Web Image Hosting Services
If your ISP doesn't give you much space on its service to post pictures of auction items, or if the thought of using FTP scares you, try some of the image hosting services that let you post auction photos for free, such as AuctionWatch (**http://www.auctionwatch.com**), MyItem.Com (**http://www.myitem.com**), or PictureBay (**http://www.picturebay.com**).

CHAPTER 10

free Stuff from the Web Sites of Major Auction Houses

You're not anticipating five-figure prices anytime soon for your cardboard box full of Avon perfume bottles, so why should you be interested in auction houses like Christie's? Because they host great Web sites. Many of the big auction houses publish regular columns and features about collecting. Some also publish catalogs of upcoming auctions. They're also great places to ogle the artifacts that win princely bids. (And you don't have to worry about your beach thongs and hockey shirt raising eyebrows when you walk in the door to browse.) After auctions are over, nearly all the houses post the winning bids on their Web sites. You can also order auction catalogs from the site and, in many cases, view them on the site.

What about bidding? Some auction houses accept absentee bids through their Web sites. That means that you place a bid prior to the auction's start by filling out a form and faxing it or e-mailing it. Many auction houses are experimenting with live auctions staged in conjunction with cyber-auction Web sites.

For instance, Sotheby's has partnered with **Amazon.Com** (**http://sothebys.amazon.com**) to put various collections designed to appeal to the computer-and-sneakers crowd, like sports memorabilia, up for bid on Amazon.Com's auction site. Phillips has hosted live Internet auctions through **The Auction Channel** (**http://www.theauctionchannel.com**).

Other smaller auction houses have been staging live auctions through Amazon.Com's **Livebid** Web site (**http://www.livebid.com**). You can read more about live Internet auctions in Chapter 5.

CHRISTIE'S
http://www.christies.com
Christie's offers news about upcoming auctions, information on how to get appraisals and the results of past auctions. In the market for a $10 million beach house? Peruse Christie's photo directory of "luxury real estate" available through Christie's.

BUTTERFIELD & BUTTERFIELD
http://www.butterfields.com

The San Francisco auction house offers oodles of good stuff on its Web site. You can read a marvelous magazine called Online Collector. It features an appraisal clinic, an ask-the-experts column, restoration help, and articles on antiques and collectibles. You can get a free appraisal of a family heirloom by filling out a form and e-mailing it to Butterfield with a scan of a photo. On the Web site you'll find additional features by clicking through categories listed under the Collecting link. You can view catalogs from upcoming and previous auctions, as well as bid through online absentee bids.

SOTHEBY'S
http://www.sothebys.com
Look under the "Collecting" feature on the Sotheby's home page for a variety of articles written for collectors by Sotheby experts. Topics range from "What Is the Significance of a Maker's Mark?" to the difference between soft and hard porcelain. You can also read details of upcoming auctions and order catalogs.

WESCHLER'S AUCTIONEERS & APPRAISERS
http://www.weschlers.com
Visit the Web site of Weschler's for an introduction to how to buy and sell at an auction.

BONHAMS
http://www.bonhams.com
One of the world's leading auctioneers, Bonhams offers free access to auction catalogues and sales information.

PHILLIPS
http://www.phillips-auctions.com/ch/index.html

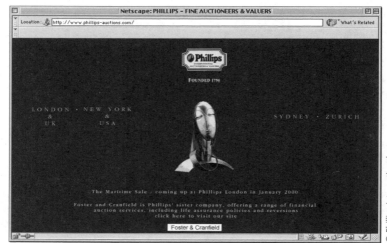

© Phillips International

SKINNER
http://www.skinnerinc.com
Skinner is the fourth largest auction house in the nation. Its Auction 101 feature tells you about the auction experience and how to buy and sell. Read articles such as a "Horse-Drawn Omnibus Toy Goes for $48,300 at Skinner." Appraisal information, online catalogs, orders, and bidding information are also available.

JONES & HORAN HOROLOGICAL AUCTIONS
http://www.jones-horan.com

Looking for Auction Catalogs? EphemerArts (**http://ephemerarts.com/catalogs.htm**) offers a huge inventory that you can browse through at their Web site. They sell catalogs from Sotheby's, Christie's, Phillips, and other auction houses, some harkening back to the early '80s.

Wondering when Sotheby's will be auctioning European paintings? Want to find out when Christie's will be auctioning clocks? **The Auction Goers Guide** (**http://www.auctiongoer.com**) chronicles upcoming auctions at major auction houses. Looking for an auction house in your area? **The Auction Guide** (**http://www.auctionguide.com**) has a database of auctions and auction houses around the United States and throughout the world.

ANTIQUORUM
http://www.antiquorum.com

Visit the Web site of watch and jewelry auction house Antiquorum to find out about future auction and read auction results.

DUPUIS JEWELLERY AUCTIONEERS
http://www.dupuisauctions.com
View pricey estate jewelry auctioned off by Dupuis.

WILLIAM DOYLE GALLERIES
http://www.doylegalleries.com
View catalogs of upcoming auctions and read bid prices from completed auctions on the Web site of Doyle Galleries.

free Web Sites of TV Shows for Collectors and Antiques Enthusiasts

What collector doesn't fantasize about stumbling onto a TV set for a show like *Antiques Roadshow* to see their crumpled heap of dishcloths salvaged from Aunt Rose's linen drawer valued at thousands of dollars by the appraisers on the couch? Alas, for most of us it will never be more than a fantasy. But it's a fun fantasy to watch played out each week on the many TV shows for collectors. The Web sites for these shows often include special features, links, and information on show segments. They're great spots to go to read up about the appraisers on the shows.

ANTIQUES ROADSHOW ON PBS
http://www.pbs.org/wgbh/pages/roadshow/home.html
This is one of Judy's mom's favorite shows. She calls her daughter regularly to say something like "I saw a beer mug on Antiques Roadshow. *It looks just like a beer mug I have. They appraised it at $30,000. Can you call PBS and try to find out more about that beer mug for me?" The PBS Web site offers tips on collectibles, an appraise-it-yourself contest, information about appraisers on this popular show, and much more.*

COLLECTING ACROSS AMERICA
http://www.collectin.com
This PBS show is hosted by Dave Maloney, author of Maloney's Antiques & Collectibles, *and Stacy Williard. They feature segments on popular types of collectibles and even offer features on collectibles for kids.*

HOME & GARDEN TV COLLECTOR'S SHOWS
http://www.hgtv.com
HGTV features a number of regular shows for collectors, including Appraisal Fair; Appraise It!; At the Auction; Collectible Treasures; *and* Restore America. *HGTV's Web site features sections where you'll find schedules and special features for each of the shows. To find them, you'll need to visit the main HGTV Web site URL listed above, because the addresses on this site change frequently.*

TREASURES IN YOUR HOME

http://www.treasuresinyourhome.com
http://www.pax.net/treasures/default.htm

Treasures In Your Home *is a relatively new collectibles show from the PAX cable network, but it already enjoys an avid following. Visit PAX's Web site to learn when it's broadcast in your community. Or, watch it on the Web through your Web browser! See the tutorial "Watch TV Shows for Collectors on the Web!"*

WATCH TV SHOWS FOR COLLECTORS ON THE WEB!

The CollectingChannel (**http://www.collectingchannel.com**) *offers live Web audio and video broadcasts of a changing roster of collectibles TV shows.*

If your local cable TV company doesn't carry your favorite collectibles show, don't despair. You might still be able to watch it through the Web. *Treasures In Your Home* is broadcast regularly on the Internet. So are several other collectibles shows.

This is how it works: You install one of the free browser plugins that plays audio and video, either RealPlayer from RealNetworks or Windows Media Player

from Microsoft. (We like to have both on hand.)
Then you tap into a broadcasting Web site like **The
CollectingChannel.Com** or **Broadcast.Com**. Click on
the broadcast link for the show you wish to see and—
voila!—the show pops up on your screen.

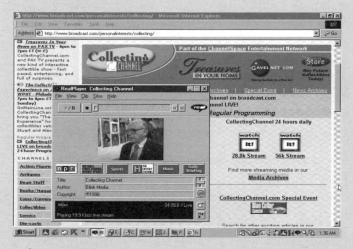

What You Need

• A 486 DX or faster PC. Macintosh users need a
Power PC 604 or better and System 8.1 or higher.
A sound card and speakers.

• A reasonably good connection to the Net. It should
be 28.8K at a minimum, but needless to say, a faster
connection is better.

• An up-to-date Web browser. Head to the Web site
of Netscape (**http://www.netscape.com**) or Microsoft
(**http://www.microsoft.com**) and download the newest
version of the one you use. You'll need a browser that
supports Java and JavaScript. Versions of Internet
Explorer prior to 5 are unable to play RealAudio files
through certain dynamic links, such as an .asp script.

• The free browser plug-in RealPlayer from
RealNetworks (**http://www.real.com**) or Windows Media

Player from Microsoft (**http://www.microsoft.com**). We like having both on our computers. Both work with both Netscape and Internet Explorer browsers.

Tips for Getting Good Sound and Pictures
• Whether you use RealPlayer or Windows Media Player, keep your multimedia plug-in current by downloading new versions from the makers' Web sites as needed. This will help insure good sound and video.

• Keep your computer's audio and video drivers current by occasionally visiting the Web site of your PC's maker and checking for any driver updates. Out-of-date audio drivers sometimes choke on compressed audio streams from broadcast Web sites.

• Clean out your browser's disk and memory caches regularly to keep audio and video error messages at bay. For instance, if your multimedia player displays an "error 14," it's usually due to a loaded cache. You might also want to increase the size of caches to handle large media files; you'll need to experiment with this. In Netscape, head to Edit/Preferences and click Advanced to expand it. Select **Cache**. In the menu on the right side of the screen, click **Clear Memory Cache** and **Clear Disk Cache**. Click **OK** and close and reload your browser. In Explorer, from the **Tools** menu, select **Internet Options** and head to the **General** tab. Under **Temporary Internet Files**, click the **Delete Files** button, then **OK**. Close and reload your browser.

• If you get "network congestion" errors, that means that either a lot of other people are on the Net or your ISP is overloaded. You may need to try watching (or listening) later in the evening when there isn't as much traffic on the Web.

• If you get timeout errors, it may be because the broadcast server is overloaded from other users. It may also be because your ISP has heavy traffic.

• If you can't connect to the broadcast server at all, it may be because many other people are trying to tap in. These broadcast sites can only handle a limited number of viewers at once.

• If sound sounds distorted when you're using RealPlayer tweak it to work more efficiently with your sound card by pulling down the **View** menu and selecting **Preferences**. Under **Sound Card Compatibility**, click the Settings button. Try selecting either **Disable 16-bit sound** or **Disable custom sampling rate**, then click **OK**. If the music doesn't sound any better try disabling the other setting. You should also take a look at the **Bandwidth** setting found in the **Connection** tab and make sure it's set to the speed of your modem.

Where to Find Live Web Broadcasts of TV Shows for Collectors

THE COLLECTINGCHANNEL.COM
http://www.collectingchannel.com

THE COLLECTING CHANNEL VIDEO ARCHIVE
http://www.collectingchannel.com/media/videoarchive.html

BROADCAST.COM
http://www.broadcast.com
http://www.broadcast.com/personalinterests/collecting

free E-zines and Magazines About Antiques & Collectibles

These days nearly every magazine has a Web site. You can read features from the magazine and even special features written especially for the Web. Many magazine Web sites also offer links to other related resources on the Internet, question-and-answer forums, and discussion groups. Magazine Web sites are great sites to bookmark and visit regularly.

This chapter includes a directory of Web sites for general interest collectibles and antiques magazines, as well as a section devoted to Web sites of specialized magazines, such as those for sports collectibles or Beanies. We've also included a directory of Web sites for general interest magazines like *Victoria* and *Country Living* that offer regular features on collectibles (and are also beautiful Web sites to read and enjoy).

Finally, we've included a guide to "e-zines," electronic magazines or newsletters, for collectors. These are free magazines or newsletters that you can read by tapping into a Web site each month or by signing up for an e-mail list. In the case of the latter, the "e-zine" will be mailed to your e-mail box each month. E-zines are usually written and published by collectible enthusiasts. They can be wonderful resources for news and gossip about the collectibles world—especially on the Internet.

Looking for Collectibles Magazines? If you're looking for magazines to subscribe to, check out **Barnes & Nobles'** magazine database and subscription service (**http://www.bn.com**). They have (we think) one of the nicest magazine selections on the Net, and also the easiest to search for publications matching your interests.

Free Web E-Zines and Newsletters

To read these free, Web-only publications, you need to tap into the Web site for the magazine, or sign up for an e-mail mailing list.

THE ANTIQUES & COLLECTING NEWSLETTER
http://collectorsweb.com/newslett.htm
Sign up for Ron McCoy's twice-monthly free e-mail newsletter which includes collectible news, reviews, guest columns, and tips on buying and selling collectibles online.

THE ATTIC MUSE: COLLECTOR'S NEWS
http://members.tripod.com/~vintage_collectibles/atticmuse.html
Antique Dealer Lee Bernstein publishes a regular e-mail newsletter with tips on buying and selling collectibles online and more. His Web site contains articles of back issues.

BOTTLE COLLECTING NEWSLETTER
http://www.antiquebottles.com/poch/index.html

Web page hosted by Reggie Lynch

This site contains the entire series of Bottle Collecting Newsletters from Glenn Poch.

MR. BILL'S DIECAST AND COLLECTIBLES NEWSLETTER
http://www.collectible-info.com/index.htm

THE COLLECTOR NEWSMAGAZINE
http://www.drspublishing.com/thecollector

Tap into the Web site of DRS Publishing to read lots and lots of wonderful articles on antiques and collectibles.

BARBARA CREWS' COLLECTIBLES CABLE AT ABOUT.COM
http://collectibles.about.com/gi/pages/mmail.htm?pid=2740&cob=home
http://www.collectibles.about.com
Subscribe to this free newsletter, from the collectibles guide at About.Com to learn about new Net links and other news in the collectibles world.

THE BARBIE DOLL NEWS FLASH
http://www.flash.net/~dsquard7/newsflash.html
Read all the latest gossip about Mattel and toy-store chains—and the inside dope about the bob haircut on Pilot Barbie!

RENEE'S JEWELRY TALK NEWS
http://gemsplusonline.com/myweb

AUTOGRAPH CENTRAL NEWSLETTER
http://www.autographcentral.com

RETRO MAGAZINE: THE MAGAZINE OF CLASSIC 20TH CENTURY POP CULTURE
http://www.retroactive.com

WORLD COLLECTORS NET MAGAZINE
http://www.worldcollectorsnet.com/magazine/index.html

ARTCULT
http://www.artcult.com/index2.htm

DOLL'ZINE
http://www.auntie.com/dollzine/main.asp

ANTIQUE JEWELRY TIMES
http://www.antiquejewelrytimes.com

BECKETT'S COLLECTIBLE REPORTS
http://www.beckett.com/news/report.asp
Read the latest on sports collectibles.

YOU MUST REMEMBER THIS— ARTICLES OF INTEREST TO COLLECTORS
http://www.remember-this.com/articles

Love Depression Glass? Sign up for The Depression Glass Shopper: The Depression Glass Supersite (**http://www.teleport.com/~dgshoppr**). You'll read tips on glass care and cleaning, online price guides, articles on many different types of collectible glass, and news about market trends in this information-packed e-zine. To read the articles you must subscribe; subscription fees start at $20/year.

◖ Web Sites for General Interest Magazines That Include Features on Antiques and Collectibles

Read features on decorating with collectibles at the Web home of Country Collectibles.

VICTORIA MAGAZINE
http://victoria.women.com/vict/index.htm

COUNTRY LIVING
http://homearts.com/cl/toc/00clhpc1.htm

COUNTRY COLLECTIBLES
http://countrycollector.com

THE HOME MONTHLY
http://www.acorn-online.com/home.htm

Peruse an extensive archive of articles from past issues, including ones on decorating with antiques, renovating historic homes, and collecting.

SOUTHERN LIVING
http://www.southernliving.com

🏺 Web Sites for General Interest Antique and Collectibles Magazines

THE FOLK ART MESSENGER
http://www.folkart.org/messenger/folkmessenger.html
Read marvelous features from issues of the magazine for the American Folk Art Society.

THE ANTIQUE TRADER ONLINE
http://www.collect.com/antiquetrader/index.html
Art & Auction *features article and news of the auction world—both in cyberspace and the real world—on its Web site.*

ART & AUCTION ONLINE
http://www.artandauction.com

ECHOES MAGAZINE
http://www.deco-echoes.com/index.html#A
Read articles from this marvelous magazine for Deco lovers.

MAINE ANTIQUE DIGEST MAGAZINE
http://www.maineantiquedigest.com

ANTIQUE & COLLECTORS REPRODUCTION NEWS
http://www.repronews.com/newsletter.html
The monthly newsletter on "fakes and reproductions."

NORTHEAST JOURNAL OF ARTS & ANTIQUES
http://www.northeastjournal.com
Read features about antiquing in Virginia and the Carolinas at the Web site of Midatlantic Antiques.

MIDATLANTIC ANTIQUES MAGAZINE
http://www.maantiques.com

THE ANTIQUE SHOPPE
http://www.antiqnet.com/antiqueshoppe

NEW YORK CITY'S ANTIQUES NEWS
http://www.nycan.com

KOVELS ON ANTIQUES & COLLECTIBLES
http://www.kovel.com

ANTIQUE WEEK ONLINE
http://www.antiqueweek.com

TRACE MAGAZINE
http://www.trace.co.uk
A magazine dedicating to locating and retrieving stolen art, antiques, and collectibles.

ANTIQUE COLLECTING — SELECTION OF ARTICLES
http://www.antiquecc.com/articles/antcol.html
http://www.antiquecc.com/articles/index.html
Information on Antique Collecting, *the journal of the Antique Collectors' Club, and an extensive selection of articles from the publication.*

KALEDEN PUBLICATION PAGES
http://www.kaleden.com/publications.html
Includes links to several antique and collectible publications, including The Antique Traveler, America's Most Wanted to Buy, Antique Week, Antiques Magazine, *and* The Vintage Times.

KRAUSE PUBLICATIONS
http://www.krause.com/magazines
A collection of collectible magazines such as World Coin News, Comic Buyer's Guide, Antique Trader Weekly, Post Card Collector, Military Trader, *and more.*

BART'S POST CARD NEWS
http://www.tias.com/mags/barr/

ANTIQUES AND THE ARTS WEEKLY
http://www.thebee.com/aweb/aa.htm

NEW ENGLAND ANTIQUES JOURNAL
http://www.antiquesjournal.com

MARTHA STEWART
http://www.marthastewart.com

FINE WOODWORKING
http://www.taunton.com

Taunton Press's magazine often includes articles on repairing and caring for wooden antiques.

Web Sites for Special Interest Antique and Collectibles Magazines

COIN WORLD ONLINE
http://www.coinworld.com
Includes an extensive library of articles.

Visit the Web site of Coin World for news and features about collecting.

JASMIN MAGAZINE
http://www.jasmin.com
Read articles from this gorgeous British magazine devoted to the art, history, and appreciation of perfumes, both current and historic.

POP CULTURE COLLECTING
http://www.odysseygroup.com/collect.htm

AMERICAN ARTIFACTS
http://www.americanartifacts.com/smma/index.htm
You can read dozens of articles about scientific and medical antiques from the magazine. Learn about microscopes used by early American agriculturists and antique surveying instruments.

BBR MAGAZINE (FOR BOTTLE COLLECTORS)
http://www.bbrauctions.co.uk/magazines.html
Read news about movie collectibles and join discussion forums at Big Reel Online.

BIG REEL: MOVIES, VIDEO & HOLLYWOOD COLLECTIBLES
http://www.csmonline.com/bigreel

DISCOVERIES
http://www.csmonline.com/discoveries
A magazine for collectors of records, CDs, and other music collectibles.

MILITARY TRADER
http://www.csmonline.com/militarytrader

POSTCARD COLLECTOR
http://www.csmonline.com/postcard

TOY TRADER
http://www.csmonline.com/toytrader

COIN WORLD
http://www.coinworld.com

LINN'S STAMP NEWS
http://www.linns.com

THE DOLL HOUSE (BARBIE)
http://www.csmonline.com/barbie

CARS & PARTS
http://www.carsandparts.com

BEANS! MAGAZINE
http://www.beansmagazine.comTUFF STUFF ONLINE:
A GUIDE TO SPORTS CARDS AND COLLECTIBLES
http://www.tuffstuffonline.com/index.html

ANTIQUE BOTTLE AND GLASS COLLECTOR MAGAZINE
http://www.glswrk-auction.com

ANTIQUE RADIO CLASSIFIED
http://www.antiqueradio.com

FIESTA COLLECTOR'S CLUB
http://www.chinaspecialties.com/fiesta.html

COIN AND CURRENCY WEEKLY
http://www.coinmall.com/ccw

Learn About the History of Film Animation at the Library of Congress
You can find out all about the history of film animation, and even view rare animation from the early days of film, at the **American Memory Project** (**http://memory.loc.org/ammem/oahtml/oahome.html**) at the Library of Congress's Web site.

free Stuff for Travelling Collectors: Guides to Antique Shops & Fleamarkets Across the Country

Ever find yourself driving down a dusty highway and wondering whether any antique shops are tucked in some nearby valley? Has business taken you to a faraway town that you know had some great collectible shops you couldn't seem to find? Life can take us to amazing places. Fortunately, antique and collectibles shops lurk in most of those places, but finding them can be hard. Phone books for major metropolitan areas often don't list antique shops tucked in country havens just outside their borders. Cab drivers, while pros at recommending raucous night spots, often fall speechless when asked the way to shops that sell perfume bottles. Guides to antique stores are popping up on the Web. Here are some to help you in your vacation planning.

FLEA MARKET DIRECTORY
http://collectors.org/doc/fleamkt.asp
A directory of markets listed by city. You'll find everything from traditional fleamarkets to farmers markets, antique markets, court days, and traders' marts.

ANTIQUE AND COLLECTIBLES GUIDE SHOP LOCATOR
http://www.ACGuide.com/ShopsLoc.html
Click on a state or country for a geographical shopping guide to antique and collectibles shops, malls, and other related businesses.

ANTIQUE AND COLLECTIBLES EVENT GUIDE
http://www.ACGuide.com/Events.html
A guide to antique and collectible events such as shows, sales, expos, and other happenings.

ANTIQUE AND COLLECTIBLES SHOW CALENDAR
http://collectors.org/doc/calendar.asp

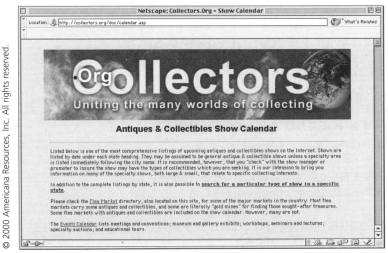

Thousands of antiques and collectibles shows sorted by state and listed by date.

ANTIQUE AND COLLECTIBLES GUIDE
SPECIALTY INDEX
http://www.ACGuide.com/Specialties.html
A guide to businesses and organizations specializing in a particular type of antique or collectible. Specialty categories are alphabetized.

MULTIDEALER ANTIQUE SHOPS, MALLS,
AND CO-OPS
http://ourworld.compuserve.com/homepages/herbbreese
Click a U.S. State or the Canada link to find an extensive listing of shops divided by city.

WHAT'S SHOWING—COLLECTIBLES
http://www.whatsshowing.on.ca/collect.html
A directory of Canadian collectible events.

ANTIQUEWEEK ONLINE CALENDARS
http://www.antiqueweek.com/cal/awcalendars.htm
This site is updated weekly with shows, auctions, and fleamarkets.

PETER WEBIT'S ANTIQUE ROAD SHOW
http://peterwebit.com/Antiques
A directory of antique dealers, markets, and shows in Ontario, Canada.

NEW ENGLAND ANTIQUE SHOWS
http://www.cjeans.com/Shows.htm

NEW ENGLAND ANTIQUE SHOPS
http://www.cjeans.com/Shoppes.htm

UPCOMING ANTIQUE SHOWS AND CONVENTIONS IN THE FLORIDA AREA
http://www.antiqnet.com/antiqueshoppe/shows/index.html

HAMPTON ROADS ANTIQUE CONNECTION
http://www.hrac.com
A Web guide to antique dealers in the Virginia cities of Norfolk, Virginia Beach, Portsmouth, Suffolk, Chesapeake, Hampton, Newport News, Yorktown, Williamsburg, and Smithfield.

NATIONAL ANTIQUE SHOP DIRECTORY
http://bestwebs.com/classifieds/index.shtml
For a fee, you can search a directory of more than 36,000 shops. If you want information for Alabama or Alaska, head over to the test drive site (http://bestwebs.com/classifieds/search.htm), where you can view the databases for free.

Ask Other Collectors on the Web for Shopping Recommendations A common topic on the antiques and collectibles mailing lists recommended in Chapter 4 is shopping recommendations for visitors to different cities. Don't be afraid to join the discussion and ask!

COLLECTOR'S UNIVERSE SHOW GUIDES
http://www.collectorsuniverse.com
Collector's Universe offers a guide to shows around the country in the following collectible interests: advertising, Americana, ancient coins, antiques, art, autographs, banknotes, beanies, books, cigars, modern coins, comic books, cowboy memorabilia, cigars, dolls, diamonds, glass, gold, silver, golf collectibles, guitars, Indian collectibles, magazines, military, minerals, movie memorabilia, paper, photographs, porcelain, pottery, political collectibles, postcards, radio & TV collectibles, science-fiction collectibles, stamps, sports, surfing collectibles, toys, sports memorabilia, watches, trains, toys, and wine.

ANTIQUE WORLD
http://www.antiquesworld.co.uk/index.html
Tap into this Web site in Britain for a guide to fairs and markets throughout the UK.

BELGIUM ANTIQUES
http://www.BelgiumAntiques.com
A directory of Belgian antique shops, dealers, auctioneers, auctions, fair, fleamarkets, and other information for travelers.

THE ANTIQUE SHOP FINDER
http://www.antique-shop.com
A database of 1,700 antique stores throughout the United States, searchable by specialty.

THE VINTAGE CLOTHING STORE WEB SITE
http://home.pacifier.com/~flapper/vintage.htm
Planning to shop for vintage clothes while on vacation? Visit this searchable database of shops around the country to find addresses, phone numbers, and other contact information for stores.

JANICE'S PERFUME BOTTLE SHOPPING PICKS
http://www.passionforperfume.com
Visit Passion for Perfume for a list of favorite shops around the U.S. that sell scrumptious perfume bottles.

ANTIQUES IN TEXAS
http://www.antiquetexas.com/index.htm
You'll find information about antiquing in Texas, with information on hundreds of dealers in several antique malls in Austin and central Texas.

ANTIQUES-SOUTHWEST
http://www.antiques-southwest.com
A guide to stores in Colorado, New Mexico, Arizona, and other parts of the southwest, it includes maps, a searchable database, and an antique show and auction calendar.

Brimfield's, the big Massachusetts antiques show, hosts a Web site where you can find directions to the show, a dealer list, and show dates (**http://www.brimfield-hotm.com**).

If you can't get there, tap into Brimfield's private auction site on eBay (**http://www.ebay.aol.com/community/library/antique-show.html**). *There you can bid on selected antiques and collectibles.*

free Web Sites of Collectors' Clubs

No matter what you collect there's probably a club for it. And chances are that they've got a Web site which offers loads of advice on every subject of interest to collectors, from storing collections to appraising and selling them.

COLLECTOR ONLINE CLUB DIRECTORY
http://www.collectoronline.com/club-directory.shtml

A directory of over 800 collector's clubs—everything from collectors of Avon products to barbed wire. You'll find e-mail contact information as well as old-fashioned postal mail contacts. The site also hosts pages for groups ranging from the American Hatpin Society to the Paperweight Collectors' Association.

ANTIQUE JOURNAL COLLECTOR CLUBS AND ORGANIZATIONS
http://www.antiqueinfo.com/journal/network.htm

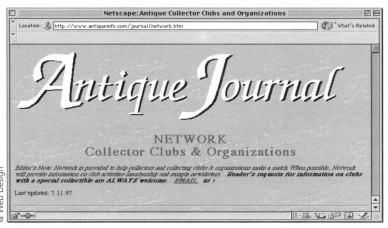

Site designed by Possibilities Unlimited Graphic & Web Design

A list of clubs and organizations, their annual dues, and contact information.

ANTIQUE WORLD'S NATIONAL CLUBS AND ASSOCIATIONS
http://www.antiqueworld.net/clubs.htm

Clubs and organizations divided into sixty categories.

Web Sites of Glass, Bottle, and Reamer Collecting Clubs

INTERNATIONAL PERFUME BOTTLE ASSOCIATION
http://www.passionforperfume.com/Ipba.HTM

VASELINE GLASS COLLECTORS, INC.
http://www.icnet.net/users/davepeterson

EARLY AMERICAN PATTERN GLASS SOCIETY
http://www.eapgs.org

NATIONAL REAMERS COLLECTORS ASSOCIATION
http://www.reamers.org

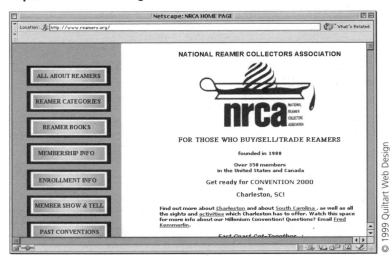

© 1999 Quiltart Web Design

THE FEDERATION OF HISTORICAL BOTTLE COLLECTORS
http://www.fohbc.com

NATIONAL MILK COLLECTORS SOCIETY
http://www.nmgcs.org

INTERNATIONAL ASSOCIATION OF PR PRUSSIA COLLECTORS, INC.
http://www.rsprussia.com

DEPRESSION GLASS AND CHINA COLLECTION CLUBS
http://www.glassshow.com/Clubs/aclubs.html

ANTIQUE & ART GLASS SALT SHAKER COLLECTORS SOCIETY
http://www.cbantiques.com/ssc

THE NATIONAL AMERICAN GLASS CLUB
http://home.att.net/~NAGC

NATIONAL DEPRESSION GLASS ASSOCIATION
http://www.glassshow.com/NDGA

INTERNATIONAL PAPERWEIGHT SOCIETY
http://paperweight.com

INTERNATIONAL PAPERWEIGHT SOCIETY
http://www.armory.com/~larry/ips.html

SWAROVSKI COLLECTORS SOCIETY
http://www.swarovski.com

 Web Sites of Military Collectible Clubs

AMERICAN SOCIETY OF MILITARY INSIGNIA COLLECTORS
http://www.asmic.org

ASSOCIATION OF AMERICAN MILITARY UNIFORM COLLECTORS
http://www.naples.net/clubs/aamuc/index.html

MILITARY COLLECTOR ASSOCIATIONS
http://www.militaria.com/assoc.html

Web Sites of Autograph and Post Card Collecting Clubs

WASHINGTON HISTORICAL AUTOGRAPH AND CERTIFICATE ORGANIZATION (WHACO)
http://www.whaco.com

An organization for collectors of historic autographs, stocks, bonds, certificates, and scripophily related items. Be sure to click the news link to read articles such as "Why Collect Historic Autographs," "Tips on Archival Framing," and "How Historic Autographs, Stocks, Bonds, and Certificates are Graded."

INTERNET POSTCARD & COLLECTIBLE CLUB
http://www.web-pac.com/mall/club

UNIVERSAL AUTOGRAPH COLLECTORS CLUB
http://www.uacc.org

Web Sites of Doll Collecting Clubs

UNITED FEDERATION OF DOLL CLUBS
http://www.ufdc.org

THE STEIFF CLUB, FOR COLLECTORS OF STEIFF BEARS
http://www.steiff-club.com

More Web Sites
for Collectors' Clubs and Societies

AMERICAN FAN COLLECTORS ASSOCIATION
http://www.fancollectors.org

INTERNATIONAL FAN COLLECTORS GUILD
http://www.hand-fan.org

ANTIQUE AND CLASSIC BOAT SOCIETY
http://www.halcyon.com/pford/acbsx.htm

THE LEGO USER'S GROUP NETWORK, OR LUGNUT
http://www.lugnet.com
This is the spot to go if you're a Lego fan. You'll find FAQs, pricing help, and tons of other information.

MUSICAL BOX SOCIETY
http://www.mbsi.org

MCDONALD'S COLLECTORS CLUB
http://www.mcdclub.com

THE RATHKAMP MATCHCOVER SOCIETY
http://www.matchcover.org

SOUTHWEST TOOL COLLECTOR'S ASSOCIATION
http://www.swtca.org
A club dedicated to the collection and appreciation of the "tools of our forefathers."

THE FOLK ART SOCIETY OF AMERICA
http://www.folkart.org/messenger/folkmessenger.html

GAR WOOD CLASSIC BOAT SOCIETY
http://www.garwood.com

INTERNATIONAL ASSOCIATION OF STUDENTS AND COLLECTORS OF HISTORIC LIGHTING
http://www.rushlight.org/index.html

ANTIQUE TELESCOPE SOCIETY
http://www1.tecs.com/oldscope

THE BEER CAN COLLECTORS OF AMERICA
http://www.bcca.com/index.html

EARLY AMERICAN INDUSTRIES ASSOCIATION
http://www.eaiainfo.org
The purpose of the EAIA is to better understand early American industries in the home, shop, and form, and to preserve tools and mechanical devices used in early America.

INTERNATIONAL SEWING MACHINE SOCIETY
http://www.ismacs.net

BREWSTER SOCIETY OF KALEIDOSCOPE ENTHUSIASTS
http://www.kaleido.com/brewster.htm

Web Sites of Jewelry and Watch Collecting Clubs

NATIONAL ASSOCIATION OF WATCH AND CLOCK COLLECTORS
http://www.nawcc.org

VINTAGE FASHION & COSTUME JEWELRY NEWSLETTER & CLUB
http://www.lizjewel.com/vf/index.htm

HATPIN COLLECTORS SOCIETY
http://members.aol.com/frankie854/index.html

THE NATIONAL CUFF LINK SOCIETY
http://www.cufflink.com

GEMOLOGICAL INSTITUTE OF AMERICA
http://www.gia.org

SOCIETY OF AMERICAN SILVERSMITHS
http://www.silversmithing.com

Web Sites of Numismatic and Bond Clubs

NUMISMATIC NETWORK CANADA
http://www.nunetcan.net
A list of organizations for those interested in coins, tokens, paper money, and related numismatic material.

SCRIPTOPHILY—THE INTERNATIONAL BOND AND SHARE SOCIETY
http://www.scripophily.org

THE AMERICAN NUMISMATIC ASSOCIATION
http://www.money.org

Stuff for Special Kinds of Collectors

No matter what you collect, there's a Web site out there to help you. In this chapter, we've assembled addresses of Web sites devoted to specific sorts of collectibles. These are sites we think are marvelous and worth reading, regardless of whether you collect the sorts of things featured on the site. On many of these Web sites, you'll find collecting news, databases of collectibles, history and restoration help, and even discussion groups.

Big Web Sites for Collectors of Sports Memorabilia

BASEBALL CARDS 1887-1914
http://memory.loc.gov/ammem/bbhtml/bbhome.html

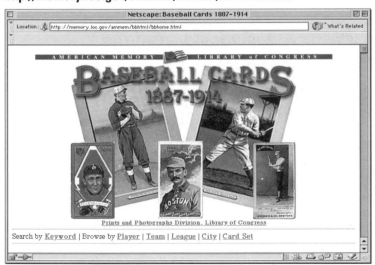

This collection from the Library of Congress includes 2,100 baseball cards dating from 1887 to 1914.

BASEBALL ALMANAC
http://baseball-almanac.com
This site is loaded with baseball facts, stories, famous firsts, historical information, autographs, and much more.

SPORTS TRADING & COLLECTING CARDS FROM ABOUT.COM
http://sportscards.about.com
Andrew Gardecki is your guide to card collecting. You'll find links to Internet resources for lovers of baseball, basketball, football, hockey, and racing cards.

JACKIE ROBINSON AND OTHER BASEBALL HIGHLIGHTS 1860S–1960S, FROM THE LIBRARY OF CONGRESS
http://memory.loc.gov/ammem/jrhtml/jrhome.html

SPORTS LEGENDS AT ABOUT.COM
http://sportslegends.miningco.com
James Alder is your guide to articles on and resources about sports memorabilia

KRAUSE PUBLICATIONS' SPORTS DIVISION
http://www.krause.com/sports
Read new articles about collecting sports memorabilia from this hobby magazine publisher.

FREQUENTLY ASKED QUESTIONS ABOUT CARDS FROM COLLECTOR LINK
http://www.collector-link.com
http://www.collector-link.com/cards/faq.shtml
Find out the best way to store cards, how much autographed cards are worth, and how cards are graded.

Looking for Web sites for collectors of animation art—or teapots—or advertising tins? Head to **Barbara Crews' Definitive Guide to Collectible Net Links at About.Com** (**http://collectibles.about.com/hobbies/collecting/col-lectibles/mlibrary.htm**). Barbara, the collectibles guide on this service, maintains a huge directory of links to Web sites related to every imaginable sort of collectible, from Precious Moments to travel souvenirs.

Big Web Sites for Comic Book Collectors

COMIC BOOK COLLECTING FROM ABOUT.COM
http://comicbooks.about.com
Stewart Brower offers feature articles, hosts chats, and tells you how to find the best information on the Net about comic collecting.

COMIC BOOK RESOURCES
http://www.comicbookresources.com
A great selection of articles, columns, news, links, and discussion boards covering the comic world, including superheros like Batman, Superman, and Spiderman.

THE COMIC PAGE
http://www.dereksantos.com/comicpage
Derek Santos offers articles on the history of comic books, and images of vintage comic ads, plus hosts message boards, and maintains a directory of Internet resources for collectors.

Check Out the Sports Collecting Newsgroups
There are a number of Usenet newsgroups devoted to collecting sports memorabilia. They are:

BASEBALL COLLECTING
rec.collecting.sport.baseball

FOOTBALL COLLECTING
rec.collecting.sport.football

HOCKEY COLLECTING
rec.collecting.sport.hockey

OTHER SPORTS COLLECTING
rec.collecting.sport.misc

You'll find directions on how to subscribe to newsgroups in Chapter 1.

Big Web Sites for Collectors of Glass

REAMERS AND DEPRESSION ERA KITCHEN GLASS
http://www.quiltart.com/judy/glass.html
Judy Smith shares pictures of her extensive collection.

SET YOUR TABLE
http://www.setyourtable.com
A directory of resources for locating, selling, and repairing discontinued and hard-to-find patterns of tableware.

"URANIUM, FLUORESCENT, AND VASELINE GLASS"
http://www.glass.co.nz/uranium.htm
The Glass Museum in New Zealand offers a beautifully illustrated article on the techniques that create this remarkable glass.

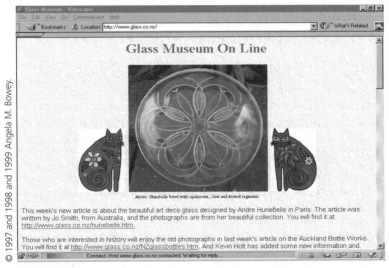

You can read many wonderful articles about glass, both modern and vintage, at The Virtual Glass Museum in New Zealand.

"EARLY AMERICAN PATTERN GLASS"
FROM THE GLASS ENCYCLOPEDIA
http://www.encyclopedia.netnz.com/eapglass.html
Pattern glass, a type of pressed glass, was manufactured in the late 19th and early 20th centuries. Read all about its different forms in this illustrated article.

To read articles about depression glass and china, visit **The Stacks** (**http://www.glassshow.com/Astack/stack.html**), an archive of articles posted to the Depression Glass Megashow site. It has articles like "Help Save the Glass and When is Rare 'Rare?'"

THE CARNIVAL GLASS FAQ, BY GLEN & STEVE THISTLEWOOD
http://www.woodsland.com/carnivalglass/faq/index.html
Carnival glass is pressed iridized glass manufactured at the beginning of the 19th century. Glen and Steve of "Carnival Central" (http://www.woodsland.com/carnivalglass/index.html) discuss the history and identification of patterns.

 ## Big Web Sites for Collectors of Vintage Clothing & Jewelry

COSTUME JEWELRY COLLECTING AT ABOUT.COM
http://costumejewels.about.com
Isabelle Bryman offers many wonderful features about vintage jewelry collecting, including an extensive collection of links to Web resources about collectibles, and information about how to buy and sell jewelry, both in cyberspace and at auctions.

EDITH WEBER'S ANTIQUE JEWELRY FAQS
http://www.antique-jewelry.com/faq.html
Find out the difference between a cameo and an intaglio, whether you should repair your grandfather's pocket watch, and what exactly a "revival" piece of jewelry is.

TIPS ON COLLECTING SPRATLING SILVER
http://www.spratlingsilver.com/tips.htm
Read about hallmarks, elements of design, and materials used in this incredible site on Spratling silver by Paula Goddard.

VINTAGE CLOTHING SERIES:
CLOTHING CARE FROM ABOUT.COM
http://reenactment.about.com/hobbies/pastimes/reenactment/librar y/weekly/aa21499.htm
Lisa Scovel and Lee Mehelis tell you whether to repair or not to, how to deal with icky odors and stains, and how to keep clothing looking good for decades. There's also information and links to other Internet resources on buying vintage, vintage for swingers, and shoes.

VICTORIAN MILLINERY—
CLEANING HATS AND TRIM
http://www.victorianmillinery.com/Cleaning.cfm
Learn how to clean felt and straw hats, plus flowers, lace, ribbons, veiling. Tips include ones on hat storage.

VINTAGE VIXEN
http://www.vintagevixen.com
Lots of advice on how to buy and store vintage clothing, plus advice for collectors. The history page details 20th century female fashion, including the 1900s Gibson Girls, 1910s Harem Chic, the 1940s war years, and more.

RETRO, THRIFT SHOPPING I
http://www.retroactive.com/tiptray/itinerant.html

RETRO, THRIFT SHOPPING II
http://www.retroactive.com/tiptray/itinerant1.html
Malvina deVries tells you how to determine whether buying some-thing is worth the effort of restoring it and how to find the best thrift stores.

VINTAGE JEWELRY ADS FROM "AUNTIE EM" AT
EMERALD CITY
http://www.emcity.com/features.htm

DOROTHY'S VINTAGE JEWELRY DESIGNER NOTES
AT EMERALD CITY
http://www.emcity.com/dorothy.htm

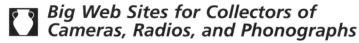

Big Web Sites for Collectors of Cameras, Radios, and Phonographs

ANTIQUE AND CLASSIC CAMERA
http://members.aol.com/dcolucci/index.html

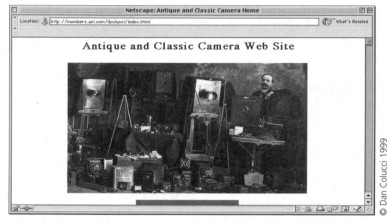

© Dan Colucci 1999

Take a look at antique cameries, plus find out about vintage camera makers and their history.

ANTIQUE PHONOGRAPH GALLERY
http://www.inkyfingers.com/Record.html

Site hosted by Rick Salsman

There's a large library of photos of phonographs including ones by Victor, Edison, Columbia, and Nipper.

VINTAGE H.H. SCOTT (VACCUM TUBE) HI-FI STEREO ARCHIVE
http://www.inquo.net/~lshuster/hhscott
This site includes information on vacuum tubes and other solid-state products not easily found elsewhere.

ANTIQUE RADIOS ONLINE
http://www.antiqueradios.com
If you love electronics which cause others to gasp, "Don't plug that in!" join other radio collecting buffs at this cyber mega-home to old radio fans.

BUYING CLASSIC COLLECTIBLE CAMERAS
http://www.photoshopper.com/editorial/collect.html
A series of articles from PhotoShopper covering a fascinating array of information. For example, did you know that patent dates on cameras are not for the camera itself but rather for some arcane features the camera utilize?

A SHORT HISTORY OF THE STEREO PHOTOGRAPH
http://gateway.eastend.com.aut/history/More.html
Ron Blum and Stephen Barnett discuss the stereoscope viewer and photographs, how they were used to record history in the making, and why they are now a very collectible item.

 Big Web Sites for Collectors of Military Memorabilia

MILITARIA.COM
http://www.militaria.com
Make this your first stop in cyberspace if you collect military memorabilia. You'll find book reviews, links to military history magazines, information on clubs devoted to military collectibles, and links to sellers of memorabilia and reproductions.

ANTIQUE GUNS
http://www.antiqueguns.com
Information for all sorts of antique gun collecting tips, including pre-Civil War, antique firearms and collectibles, parts, and more.

⬤ Big Web Sites for Collectors of Movie & TV Memorabilia

CLASSIC TV FROM ABOUT.COM
http://classictv.about.com
Debi Jenkins is your guide to feature articles, a classic TV newsletter and bulletin board, classic TV chat, and links to all your favorite classic TV shows from the Addams Family *and* I Love Lucy *to the* Twilight Zone *and* Wild Wild West.

MOVIE AND TV EPHEMERA/MEMORABILIA FROM SUITE 101
http://www.suite101.com/welcome.cfm/ephemera_memorabilia
John McGarvey is your guide to a collection of articles and links.

TV TOYS LIBRARY — POP CULTURE COLLECTING
http://www.tvtoys.com/library/index.html
A selection of articles from Pop Culture Collecting, *including "The View from Waltons' Mountain," "The Days of Dallas," and "A Very Brady Collection."*

Visit the world of TVToys.Com for features and ephemera from shows like the Flying Nun *and the* Dukes of Hazzard.

 **Big Web Sites for**
Other Types of Collectors

"COLLECTING TOOLS—WHY?"
http://www.tooltimer.com/collecting.htm

UNION HILL ANTIQUE TOOLS DATABASE OF TOOLS
http://www.tooltimer.com/tools.htm
Union Hill Antique Tools offers a helpful essay for the beginning tool collector, plus links and other advice. Union Hill also offers an e-mail discussion list for antique tool collectors.

AUTOGRAPH CENTRAL
http://www.autographcentral.com
You'll find everything for the beginning autograph hound, from links to Web resources to help on authenticating autographs— even a database of scans of famous autographs that you can compare yours to.

THE ELECTRONIC NEANDERTHAL
http://www.cs.cmu.edu/~alf/en/en.html
If you collect old tools or restore antique furniture, start your surf-ing at the Electronic Neanderthal, where you'll find links to wood-working sites and tool collectors around the Web.

And you thought you were the only one who collected old wooden woodworking vises!

"ANTIQUE MAPS: A COLLECTOR'S HANDBOOK" BY CARL MORELAND AND DAVID BANNISTER

http://www.antiquemaps.co.uk/book

Read the entire book online to learn about the history of maps and sea charts, the printing of maps and playing cards, different map makers around the world, and how to get started collecting maps.

PRIMARILY PETROLIANA OLD GAS STATION COLLECTIBLES

http://www.oldgas.com

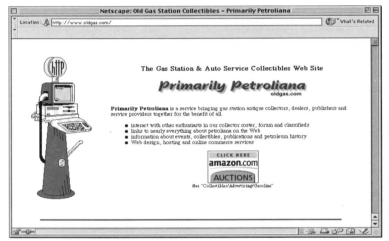

Some of the many features of this site from Jim Potts include swap meets and auctions, a gas-station shop talk forum, and an extensive listing of roadside and automotive web sites.

THE SCIENTIFIC AND MEDICAL ANTIQUE COLLECTING GUIDE

http://www.utmem.edu/personal/thjones/sci_ant.htm
http://www.utmem.edu/personal/thjones/onlinere.htm

Thinking of starting a collection of old stethoscopes? Wondering if you should throw out grandpa's old microscope or enshrine it in the china hutch? This wonderful Web site by Thomas E. Jones will tell you everything you need to know to get started collecting. Plus it includes links to hundreds of sites around the Internet where you can learn more about the history of scientific instruments, and view the collections of research institutions around the world.

free Stuff for Doll & Other Toy Collectors

Toys can remind us of the happiest moments of our lives. Will you ever forget that Christmas your parents gave you a remote control model airplane or that special pajama-bag doll? Toys can remind us of our fantasies. Maybe you'll never be an Amazon like Xena, but you can pose a Xena action figure on your china hutch. That's some consolation. It's no wonder that toys are among the most popular of collectibles. There are literally tens of thousands of Web sites devoted to toy collecting. There are Web sites for Barbies, Beanies, Big Wheels, and every possible species of action figure. There are even Web sites for yo-yo aficionados. Here is a guide to some of the biggest toy collecting Web sites. Use them as a springboard to find Web sites devoted to your favorite toy.

 Big Web Sites for Doll Collectors

BARBIE® DOLL COLLECTING AT ABOUT.COM
http://barbiedolls.about.com
Sarah Locker is your host for weekly articles, a newsletter, a chat room for Barbie lovers, and lots of links to other Web resources devoted to America's favorite doll.

MATTEL'S BARBIE®.COM
http://www.barbie.com/collectors
Mattel's official collecting site includes fun facts, tips and glossary, frequently asked questions, and collector terminology like "NRFB," which means it was "never removed from box."

DOLL COLLECTING AT ABOUT.COM
http://collectdolls.about.com
Denise Van Patten leads you to all the best Web sites for collecting vinyl, cloth, porcelain and paper dolls. She includes a great section on restoration and repair advice. She offers display advice and much more. This should be your first stop if you're a doll collector!

KAYLEE'S KORNER—
THE DOLL COLLECTION CONNECTION
http://www.dollinfo.com/index.html
There are message boards for doll collectors, an e-mail newsletter, a doll of the month, lots of advice and fun, and a huge directory of Web resources about dolls.

GARY'S TIPS ON DOLL COLLECTING
http://www.sowatzka.com/gary/tips.htm
Gary Sowatzka tells you how to get started collecting dolls. He tells you about different sorts of vintage dolls, including composition, bisque, French bisque, German bisque, glazed china heads, untinted bisque, paper mache and wax ones.

RAGGEDY LAND — THE RAGGEDY ANN AND
ANDY HOME PAGE
http://www.raggedyland.com

YO JOE—THE 3³/₄" G.I. JOE COLLECTOR'S SITE
http://www.yojoe.com

DOLL COLLECTING AT COLLECTOR'S UNIVERSE
http://www.collectors.com/dolls

Collector's Universe offers some captivating articles on dolls, plus price guides and a guide to shows around the country.

FIGURES.COM
http://www.figures.com
Read breaking news and features and access an action figure database.

ACTION GIRL'S GUIDE TO FEMALE FIGURES
http://users.aol.com/sarahdyer
Comic-book artist Sarah Dyer shares an amazing list of almost every female action figure made in the USA.

ACTION FIGURE TIMES
http://www.primenet.com/~btn/aft.html
Plenty of news, tips, and features about action figure toy collecting.

THE BEGINNER'S GUIDE TO ACTION FIGURE COLLECTING
http://www.toymania.com/beginnersguide
Learn about the 10 rules of acquisition, a collector's crash course, toy tracking tactics, and more from Eric G. Myers, Jason A. Geyer, and the Raving Toy Mania.

FLOSSY'S DOLL AND TOY COLLECTIBLES
http://www.youfoundme.com/flossy.htm

© Flossy Eddy 1996.

You'll find a doll glossary, doll care hints, e-mail discussion groups, chat area, a doll newsletter, and lots more.

 **Big Web Sites for Beanie Babies® Collectors**

VIRTUAL BEANIE BABIES®
http://www.virtualbeaniebabies.com
Beanie price lists, features, animated Beanies, Beanie birth dates, Beanie cards you can send to your friends. And more!

TY—BEANIE BABIES® OFFICIAL CLUB
http://www.ty.com
This is the official site of Beanie Babies. It offers a list of current and retired Beanie Babies.

BEANIEMOM NEWSLETTER
http://www.beaniemom.com
Learn about Beanie prices, mistagged Beanies, tag cover-ups, and a whole lot more.

DAILY BEAN NEWS AND RUMORS
http://www.dailybean.com
Wondering why Beanie Mom's announcement that Snowboy's real name could be Snowy caused a panic? This site offers the scoop on the latest news and rumors.

 More Big Web Sites for Toy Collectors

TOYCOLLECTING AT ABOUT.COM
http://toycollecting.about.com
Gianfranco Origliato is your guide for price guides, features, and links to discussion groups about Japanese toys, bears, kites, beanies, Furbies, Star Wars collectibles, and more.

KIDS COLLECTING AT ABOUT.COM
http://www.kidscollecting.about.com
Robert Olson is your guide to Pokémon, American Girls, Beanies, bears, yo-yos, Boy Scout merit badges, and more.

CHRIS DOYLE'S ISLAND OF BOOTLEG TOYS
http://home.earthlink.net/~cjdoyle
An entertaining look at bootleg toys, including a fascinating FAQ.

Tap into The Big Red Toybox for features about your favorite toy collectibles.

THE BIG RED TOYBOX
http://www.bigredtoybox.com
Among the marvels on this huge Web site for toy collectors is a "toy locator" database, into which you can type a type of toy. Select the manufacturer and the site will tell you what they think the toy is.

THE STAR WARS COLLECTORS ARCHIVE
http://www.toysrgus.com

THE DELAWARE TOY AND MINIATURE MUSEUM
http://thomes.net/toys
Learn about this non-profit museum and view photos of some of its collection of miniatures, dollhouses, and toys dating from 1770 to 1960.

RAVING TOY MANIAC:
THE MAGAZINE FOR YOUR INNER CHILD
http://www.toymania.com

Jeff Cope, Mike Fichera, Eric G. Myers, and Jason A. Geyer maintain this amazing Web site, packed with toy collecting advice and articles. Read about action figures, visit the Cool Toy Site of the Week, and much more at the Raving Toy Maniac, one of the best toy sites on the Web.

TWO KIDS AND A GROWNUP
http://www.mindspring.com/~tmp95

This site includes a newbie's guide to toys, answering questions such as "What's a tootsietoy?"

THE YO-YO PAGE
http://www.socool.com/yopage.html

DIE CAST COLLECTORS RESOURCE PAGE
http://ourworld.compuserve.com/homepages/ppro/index.html

free Stuff for Money & Stamp Collectors

If you collect money rather than spend it, we recommend you start your Internet adventures at the **Paper Money WWW Directory** (**http://web.idirect.com/~mjp/mjpwww.html**). This must-bookmark site offers a huge directory of links to Internet resources related to collecting money from different nations, as well as dealers, organizations, and even software. If you're a coin collector, head to **Goldsheet Numismatic Directory** (**http://goldsheet.simplenet.com/coins.htm**), where you'll find over 1,300 links to coin collecting information around the Internet.

If you collect stamps, head to **Stamp Collecting at About.Com** (**http://collectstamps.about.com**) Michael Mills offers collecting hints, tips, and articles, plus links to resources around the Net. You can sign up for a newsletter, participate in chats, and read about stamp news from around the world.

More Web Sites for Money Collectors

RON WISE'S WORLD PAPER MONEY HOMEPAGE
http://aes.iupui.edu/rwise
Ron features photos of over 2,000 notes on his site, which is dedicated to his golden retriever.

PAPER MONEY COLLECTING FAQ
http://www.members.home.net/giese1/pfaq.html

PAPER MONEY DEALERS BY BRUCE GIESE
http://www.members.home.net/giese1/dealers.html
Bruce maintains this site, which is a compilation of wisdom shared in the Usenet newsgroup rec.collecting.paper-money.

BANKNOTES, PAPER MONEY & BONDS
http://sammler.com/coins/banknote.htm
You'll find frequently asked question files that will fill you in on everything you need to know about collecting currency and determining its value.

COIN COLLECTING FAQ, PART 1, PART 2, AND PART 3
http://www.telesphere.com/ts/coins/faq.html
http://www.telesphere.com/ts/coins/faq2.html
http://www.telesphere.com/ts/coins/gloss.html
Lots of advice covering topics, such as what coins are worth; how to get started collecting; how to handle coins; and coin grading, pricing and storage. Part 3 of this FAQ is a glossary of numismatic terms.

THE U.S. GOVERNMENT'S BUREAU OF ENGRAVING AND PRINTING
http://www.bep.treas.gov

Did you know that the U.S. government issued paper currency in denominations below $1 during the Civil War because metal was needed for the war? Learn the history of why certain individuals are pictured on paper currency. Tap into the Kid's Page for history and trivia on U.S. currency and find lots of stamp collecting information.

Tap into Usenet Money Collecting Newsgroups
There are two excellent discussion groups for collectors on Usenet: for coin collecting, **rec.collecting.coins**, and for paper money, **rec.collecting.paper-money**. For directions on how to join them, head to Chapter 1.

More Web Sites for Stamp Collectors

STAMP SITES.COM
http://www.stampsites.com

At this great Web site by Linn's Stamp News, you'll find links to over 18,000 stamp-related Web pages around the world.

THE STAMP TRADERS LIST
http://www.stamptraderlist.dk
Phil Guptill and Hans Mortensen run this huge world-wide stamp trading bulletin board in Denmark.

THE HISTORY OF STAMPS
http://sammler.com/stamps/history.htm
Did you know that the first official central royal mail office was opened in England in 1516? This site provides an overview of stamp history and the first issues of stamps, as well as answering readers' questions.

INDEX

For more information on other fine books from C&T Publishing, write for a free catalog:

C&T Publishing, Inc., P.O. Box 1456, Lafayette, CA 94549

(800) 284-1114

http://www.ctpub.com   e-mail: ctinfo@ctpub.com

ABOUT THE AUTHORS

Judy Heim is a self-described eBay addict who as written about online auctions and the collectibles scene on the Net for national magazines since the inception of eBay. She's the author or co-author of 14 computer books, including *The Needlecrafter's Computer Companion*. She's written for *PC World* magazine for 15 years, and for 10 years authored a monthly Internet column for the magazine. She has written for *Family Circle*, *CNN Interactive*, *Newsweek*, *Cosmopolitan*, *PC/Computing*, *Family PC*, and many other magazines. She collects dolls and vintage clothing, and is an avid furniture restorer.

Gloria Hansen (when not on the Internet) frequents fleamarkets and antique shops and collects vintage fabric, sewing equipment, coins, and other things that take up too much space. Gloria is also an award-winning craftsperson, and her work has appeared in numerous magazines, books, and on television. She has written articles for leading computer magazines and craft publications, and she writes the "High-Tech Quilting" column for *The Professional Quilter*. She is the co-author of seven other Internet and computer-related books. You can visit her Web page at **http://www.gloriahansen.com**. Gloria lives in East Windsor Township, New Jersey.

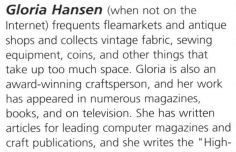

BIBLIOGRAPHY

Heim, Judy and Gloria Hansen, *Free Stuff for Quilters*, C&T Publishing, Concord, CA,1998

_____. *Free Stuff for Crafty Kids* C&T Publishing, Concord, CA,1999

_____. *Free Stuff for Sewing Fanatics*, C&T Publishing, Concord, CA,1999

_____. *Free Stuff for Stitchers*, C&T Publishing, Concord, CA,1999

_____. *The Quilters Computer Companion*, No Starch Press, San Francisco, CA, 1998

Heim, Judy, *The Needlecrafter's Companion*, No Starch Press, San Francisco, CA, 1999

FREE STUFF ON THE INTERNET SERIES

Free Stuff for Crafty Kids
Includes Web sites that offer kid-friendly projects, such as origami, kites, sewing, rubber stamps, holiday crafts, cartooning, and more.

Free Stuff for Sewing Fanatics
Free stuff for all kinds of sewing topics, including sewing machine help, dollmaking, serging, and patterns, and bridal sewing.

Free Stuff for Stitchers
An up-to-date list of sites that offer the best free stuff for stitchers, knitters, and beaders! More advice than you could read in a lifetime.

Free Stuff for Quilters, 2nd Edition
Over 150 updated new links on quilt patterns, discussion groups, and organizations, plus quilt shops to visit, how-tos, and galleries of textiles and fiber arts.

Free Stuff for Gardeners
Web sites for everything gardening related, including tips, tree advice, ponds, landscaping, and help for growing roses, bulbs, or vegetables.

 **www.ctpub.com**